THE THEATRE
OF
MEYERHOLD
AND
BRECHT

RECENT TITLES IN
CONTRIBUTIONS IN DRAMA AND THEATRE STUDIES
SERIES EDITOR: JOSEPH DONOHUE

Theatrical Touring and Founding in North America
L. W. Conolly, editor

Bernhardt and the Theatre of Her Time
Eric Salmon, editor

Revolution in the Theatre: French Romantic Theories of Drama
Barry V. Daniels

Serf Actor: The Life and Career of Mikhail Shchepkin
Laurence Senelick

Musical Theatre in America: Papers and Proceedings of the Conference on the Musical Theatre in America
Glenn Loney, editor

Garrick Claims the Stage: Acting as Social Emblem in Eighteenth-Century England
Leigh Woods

A Whirlwind in Dublin: *The Plough and the Stars* Riots
Robert G. Lowery, editor

German Actors of the Eighteenth and Nineteenth Centuries: Idealism, Romanticism, and Realism
Simon Williams

William Archer on Ibsen: The Major Essays, 1889–1919
Thomas Postlewait, editor

Theatre for Working-Class Audiences in the United States, 1830–1980
Bruce A. McConachie and Daniel Friedman, editors

Hamlet on Stage: The Great Tradition
John A. Mills

America's Musical Stage: Two Hundred Years of Musical Theatre
Julian Mates

From Farce to Metadrama: A Stage History of *The Taming of the Shrew*, 1594–1983
Tori Haring-Smith

THE THEATER OF MEYERHOLD AND BRECHT

Katherine Bliss Eaton

Contributions in Drama and Theatre Studies, Number 19

GREENWOOD PRESS
Westport, Connecticut • London, England

Library of Congress Cataloging in Publication Data

Eaton, Katherine Bliss.
  The theater of Meyerhold and Brecht.

  (Contributions in drama and theatre studies,
ISSN 0163-3821 ; no. 19)
  Bibliography: p.
  Includes index.
  1. Meĭerkhol'd, V. E. (Vsevolod Emil'evich), 1874–
1940—Influence. 2. Brecht, Bertolt, 1898–1956—
Sources. 3. Theater—Production and direction.
I. Title. II. Series.
PN2728.M4E28 1986   832'.912   85-9910
ISBN 0-313-24590-8 (lib. bdg. : alk. paper)

Library of Congress Catalog Card Number: 85-9910
ISBN: 0-313-24590-8
ISSN: 0163-3821

First published in 1985

Greenwood Press
A division of Congressional Information Services, Inc.
88 Post Road West
Westport, Connecticut 06881

Printed in the United States of America

The paper used in this book complies with the
Permanent Paper Standard issued by the National
Information Standards Organization (Z39.48-1984).

10 9 8 7 6 5 4 3 2 1

Copyright Acknowledgments

"Is the People Infallible," from *Bertolt Brecht: Poems, 1913-1956*, 2d ed., ed. John
Willett and Ralph Manheim (London: Methuen, 1979), is reprinted with permission.
Every reasonable effort has been made to trace the owners of copyright materials
in this book, but in some instances this has proven impossible. The publishers
will be glad to receive information leading to more complete acknowledgments
in subsequent printings of the book and in the meantime extend their apologies
for any omissions.

For Henry L. Eaton

I also met German writers, including Brecht, sensitive and astute. He talked about death, about Meyerhold's productions, about agreeable trifles.

Ilya Ehrenburg
Memoirs: 1921–1941

CONTENTS

Illustrations ix
Acknowledgments xi
Introduction 1
1. Brecht's Contacts with the Theater of Meyerhold 9
2. "Everyone Sees Me and I See Everyone" 49
3. "The Actors Were Served Up in Portions on Small Platform-Plates" 77
4. "A Demonstratively Proletarian Shabbiness" 91
5. Conclusions: A Trojan Horse 117
Bibliography 125
Index 137

ILLUSTRATIONS

1. Portrait of Vsevolod Meyerhold
2. Bertolt Brecht
3. A scene from Meyerhold's production of *Roar, China!* (1926), by Sergei Tretiakov. Realistically dressed coolies pull their heavy load in front of an abstract setting.
4. A scene from Brecht's production of *Mother Courage and Her Children* (1953). Realistically dressed peasants pull their heavy load in front of an abstract setting. Helene Weigel as Mother Courage, Angelika Hurwicz as Kattrin, Ernst Kahler as Eilif, and Hannes Fischer as Schweizerkas.
5. Meyerhold's *Woe to Wit* (1928), by Aleksandr Griboedov. The Dining Room Episode.
6. Brecht's production of *Herr Puntila and His Man Matti* (1948). The Dining Room Episode.
7. Two doomed wise men: Azdak (played by Ernst Busch) in Brecht's production of *The Caucasian Chalk Circle* (1954) and Sergei Tretiakov, 1927.

ACKNOWLEDGMENTS

I am grateful to Professor Reinhold Grimm for suggesting a paper on Mayakovsky and Brecht, which led to this monograph.

The Wisconsin Alumni Research Foundation, the International Research and Exchanges Board, and the University of Illinois Russian and East European Center's program of summer fellowships helped support my research. I also wish to acknowledge the work of Phyllis Eccleston, who typed the final draft.

My greatest debt is to my husband, who has been an unfailing source of encouragement and practical advice. He spent many hours editing, proofreading, and typing the various drafts of this work.

Parts of Chapter 1 were published in *Comparative Drama* (Spring 1977), and in the *Brecht-Jahrbuch* (1979).

I alone am responsible for any mistakes.

THE THEATER
OF
MEYERHOLD
AND
BRECHT

INTRODUCTION

The search for origins in the history of ideas is unending. There are always prior and parallel developments. The history of avant-garde theater can be traced to the eighteenth century and the dramatic principles of Lessing and Goethe, or it can be traced to Thespis, who is said to have separated the actor from the chorus. Though Bertolt Brecht is the theater worker most closely associated with the "epic" style of theater that emerged in Germany in the 1920s, he naturally owed much to his predecessors and contemporaries. For Brecht as for other pioneers of the avant-garde theater of the time, the most important source of ideas and inspiration was probably engendered in the work of the Russian Vsevolod E. Meyerhold. Though most famous as a director, Meyerhold's method of radically reworking texts to suit his purposes entitled him to wear the playwright's hat as well. And words were only the beginning. He had a vocabulary of movement, rhythm, and color "which speaks to the eyes in the same way that the text addresses the ears."[1]

In 1899 Meyerhold, a twenty-five-year-old actor with the Moscow Art Theater, was distressed that Art Theater actors under Nemirovich-Danchenko were not given the opportunity to become thoroughly informed about their roles. Meyerhold thought Nemirovich-Danchenko and Stanislavsky ought to meet regularly with their actors in order to discuss and debate all aspects of a performance. These talks would not only enhance the productions, they would benefit the intellectual and moral life of the actors. "Do we actors really need *only* to act?" Meyerhold asked Danchenko. "On the contrary, what we want is to *think* while acting." The young actor went on to explain that he and his colleagues needed to understand the play and the playwright socially and psychologically, in order to *"consciously* express the ideas of the author, and . . . *consciously* relate to the play and the public."[2]

Meyerhold never gave up the idea that it is important for performers to be aware of the social and psychological implications of the performance. Walter Benjamin, one of Brecht's closest friends as well as one of his earliest explicators, noted that Meyerhold's actors were unique because they could simultaneously perform and think.[3] From the thinking actor to the thinking spectator is a short but crucial step which completes the circle of mutual interaction and creativity. If Meyerhold often seemed too "intellectual" for his audiences, it was because he expected from them a creative effort to match his own.

The poet Mayakovsky was Meyerhold's close friend, protégé, and collaborator. The prologue of Mayakovsky's play *Mystery-Bouffe* (1918) is a statement of theatrical principles which Meyerhold had espoused as early as 1905.

> The stage, you know,
> is only one-third of the hall. Therefore,
> at an interesting show,
> if things are set up properly,
> your pleasure is multiplied by three.
> But if the play isn't interesting,
> then you're wasting your time
> looking at even one-third of what's happening.
> For other theatrical companies
> the spectacle doesn't matter:
> for them
> the stage
> is a keyhole without a key.
> "Just sit there quietly," they say to you,
> "either straight or sidewise,
> and look at a slice of other folks' lives."

> We, too, will show you life that's real—very!
> But life transformed by the theater into a spectacle
> most extraordinary.[4]

The idea that Meyerhold influenced Western avant-garde theater in general and Brecht in particular is not new. In the 1920s and 1930s, when Meyerhold flourished, before he and his name disappeared, à la Stalin, that idea was current. But it was also denied. From Brecht's early mentor Erwin Piscator, for example: "Of course we all looked to Russia just then, of course we were all anxious to know about everything going on in the Soviet Union. But must we just for that be stamped imitators of the Meyerholds and the Tairovs? . . . The fact is that certain things in every era are in the air."[5] Piscator's widow later repeated this denial on the grounds that her husband did not see a Meyerhold production until 1930, by which time he had already developed his own style.[6] But Julius Bab, a leading theater critic and perhaps the most knowledgeable chronicler of German theater from 1900 to 1935, believed that Meyerhold had directly affected the development of avant-garde theater in the West. In his 1928 study of contemporary theater (which includes descriptions and photographs of Meyerhold's productions) Bab pointed out that Piscator as well as such other Brecht associates as Berthold Viertel, George Grosz, and Caspar Neher, were indebted either to Meyerhold or to modernist Russian theater.[7] This view did not spring from any wishful thinking. In fact, the German critic was apprehensive that the Russians, with their love of visual devices and aversion to psychologizing, might dehumanize theater.

Henri Guilbeaux (an early publicizer of Meyerhold in Germany) observed in 1930 that "it does not do injustice to Piscator to say that he was influenced by Meyerhold." Guilbeaux saw Piscator's theater as a mixture of "unemancipated naturalism, of Meyerhold and of Proletcult," and went on to say "it is certain" that in his staging of The Threepenny Opera (1928) and The Pioneers of Ingolstadt (1929) at the Schiffbauerdamm Theater (Berlin) Brecht was the beneficiary of Meyerhold's work, "and only a vain man would feel himself diminished by this. . . . The acrobatics, the dynamism, the projections of various information on a screen, certain theatrical trouvailles are from Meyerhold-

ism.''[8] Guilbeaux further remarked that those who have borrowed from Meyerhold always protest they never saw
Meyerhold's productions until these were brought west in 1930.
In answer, Guilbeaux pointed out that long before the 1930 tour,
journals in Europe and America not only reported on Meyerhold's troupe but also published photographs of most of his
mises en scène presented in Moscow. Secondly, Guilbeaux argued, even though the Meyerhold theater did not tour until
April 1930, Tairov's ensemble twice visited Berlin in 1923, and
"Meyerhold created Tairov."[9] Finally there is "above all, word-
of-mouth information: one cannot count the number of Germans
who have travelled in Russia, nor the number of Soviets so-
journing abroad who have reported with ample detail the basic
principles of the ideas and inventions of the Meyerhold theater."[10] Guilbeaux modestly failed to mention his own early (1922)
and prophetic German essay on Meyerhold in which he carefully
described Meyerhold's use of costuming, pantomime, and techniques borrowed from the circus and medieval folk theater. He
also showed how Meyerhold located *The Magnanimous Cuckold*
outside time and place in order to universalize it.[11]

Thus, at least by 1922, and with increasing regularity thereafter, Germany had news about the new Soviet theater. Even
in far-off America, by the mid-1920s Meyerhold's name and accomplishments were household knowledge to theater people,
who as yet (and for many years to come) knew nothing of Bertolt
Brecht.[12] Why, then, are Brecht's dramatic theory and style,
which in every important detail so clearly echo Meyerhold's
work, now popularly seen as phenomena which either sprang
fresh and whole from Brecht's imagination, or in some vague
and peripheral way were influenced by Greek theater, Renaissance theater, medieval theater—in other words, anything and
everything but the work of Vsevolod Meyerhold? Perhaps the
answer lies in the power of Stalin's purges, which erased not
only the mortal part of so many millions of people, but in the
case of artists, attempted to destroy their fame as well.

Between 1939 (the year of his arrest) and 1956 (the year of his
"rehabilitation") Meyerhold's renown nearly vanished. Important writing on Meyerhold began anew with the publication of

John Willett's *The Theatre of Bertolt Brecht* (1959). Willett reminded people of the close ties between Germany and Russia from the early part of the century until 1933, and of the parallels between the work of Brecht and Meyerhold. Willett also suggested that Brecht's famous theory of the "Alienation Effect" (*Verfremdungs-effekt*, or V-Effect) may have been derived from the concept of *ostranenie* (estrangement) developed by the Russian Formalist critic Viktor Shklovsky.[13]

The rehabilitation of Meyerhold and other Russian artists and intellectuals of the 1920s and 1930s has reminded the world of the remarkable accomplishments of Soviet art in those decades. More than that, it has led to a rediscovery of the considerable influence that early twentieth-century Russian art had on the West. In the particular case of Meyerhold and Brecht, the argument dismissing similarities between their work as merely interesting coincidences is no longer persuasive.[14] There are too many similarities, representing every important aspect of their dramatic art, from theoretical foundations to the use of stage props. And if Brecht never admitted to Meyerhold's direct influence, that should not close off speculation on the matter—artistic ideas are not obliged to travel directly. Furthermore, the contention that Meyerhold did influence Brecht (and that is a principal theme in this work) should not be taken as an attempt to downgrade Brecht. Among his various talents, Brecht was, like most great artists, a "great" borrower.

Nevertheless, the brief I hold here is for Meyerhold: that he is one of the great twentieth-century directors, that he was at the heart of a dramatic renaissance which, surviving repression, murder, and exile, altered the course of modern theater, and that many inventions attributed to Brecht are clearly evident in Meyerhold's earlier theatrical work. But as I said at the beginning of this introduction, there is a serious pitfall in assigning origins—they keep slipping further into the past. So the question of who did what first is cover for the real aims of this study: to help restore Meyerhold to his deserved place in the history of art, and, through a study of the two directors, to provide a basic guide to the theory and practice of Meyerhold. And if I'm not far wrong, to the theater of Brecht, as well.

NOTES

1. Charles Dullin, *Souvenirs et notes de travail d'un acteur* (Paris: O. Lieutier, 1946). Cited in: John Gassner, *Form and Idea in Modern Theater* (New York: Holt, Rinehart and Winston, 1956), p. 197.
2. Vsevolod E. Meierkhol'd, *Perepiska 1869–1939* (Moscow: Iskusstvo, 1976), pp. 20–21.
3. Walter Benjamin, *Understanding Brecht*, trans. Anna Bostock (London: NLB, 1973), pp. 10–11.
4. Vladimir Mayakovsky, "Prologue" to *Mystery-Bouffe*, in *The Complete Plays of Vladimir Mayakovsky*, trans. Guy Daniels (New York: Washington Square Press, 1968), pp. 45–47.
5. Erwin Piscator, *Schriften*, 2 vols., ed. Ludwig Hoffmann, (Berlin: 1968), 2:266. Cited in: Marjorie L. Hoover, *Meyerhold: The Art of Conscious Theater* (Amherst: University of Massachusetts Press, 1974), pp. 261–62.
6. Maria Ley-Piscator, *The Piscator Experiment: The Political Theatre* (New York: J. Heineman, 1967), pp. 74–75.
7. Julius Bab, *Das Theater der Gegenwart: Geschichte der dramatischen Bühne seit 1870* (Leipzig: J. J. Weber, 1928), pp. 192, 219, 221–29.
8. Although Jacob Geis was the official director of *The Pioneers of Ingolstadt*, Brecht controlled the production.
9. Aleksandr Tairov (1885–1950) acted under Meyerhold's direction in 1906 and in 1914 founded his own ensemble, the Kamerny Theater, "with aims close to Meyerhold's." The two men eventually became bitter enemies. See Hoover, *Meyerhold*, pp. 252–54.
10. Henri Guilbeaux, "Meyerhold et les tendances du théâtre contemporain," *Les humbles* 15 (May-June 1930): 21–23. "Guilbeaux (1884) was a representative of the French wing of Futurism-Dynamism. . . . In 1919 he went to the Soviet Union and worked until 1924 for the Commissariat of Enlightenment," according to Fritz Mierau, "Die Rezeption der Sowjetischen Literatur in Deutschland 1920–24," *Zeitschrift für Slawistik* 3 (1958): 622. Despite all the evidence to the contrary, the argument that Meyerhold's ideas did not reach Germany or Piscator until 1930, persists in C. D. Innes's *Erwin Piscator's Political Theater: The Development of Modern German Drama* (Cambridge: Cambridge University Press, 1972), p. 186. In 1928, Julius Bab commented on Piscator's production of *Die Räuber* (1926): "Basically it was a very talented piece of work of the Russian school. It was presented as Communist propaganda theater, with just that same disregard for the poet's text proclaimed by Meyerhold" (Bab, 224). Professor Herbert Marshall sent me a copy of a 1928 letter from the Volksbühne Associations which discusses the

Russian influence on Piscator (Herbert Marshall Archives; Huntly Carter Section). Artur Kutscher, a professor of contemporary German literature, whose seminars Brecht attended during his student days in Munich, wrote that "The Russians struck the fetters from the theatre. [This is an allusion to Tairov's book *Unfettered Theater* (*Das entfesselte Theater*) which had been published in Germany in 1923.] Piscator adopted their methods, improved upon them and enlarged them in the matter of engineering and machinery." "The German Theatre," *Theatre Arts Monthly* 17 (February 1933): 129.

11. Guilbeaux, "Der *Cocu magnifique*, der Regisseur Meyerhold und die neue Dramaturgie in der RSFSR," *Das literarische Echo* 24 (15 July 1922): 1217–21.

12. John Fuegi, "Russian 'Epic Theatre' Experiments and the American Stage," *The Minnesota Review*, New Series 1 (Fall 1973): 102–12. According to Efim Etkind, "There was a time in the 1920s when Brecht was well-known in Russia." See his "Brecht and the Soviet Theater," in *Bertolt Brecht: Political Theory and Literary Practice*, ed. Betty Nance Weber and Hubert Heinen (Athens: The University of Georgia Press, 1980), p. 82.

13. 3rd rev. ed. (New York: New Directions, 1968), pp. 110–12, 206–07, 209.

14. In her monograph on Meyerhold, Hoover asserts that "Brecht did not 'borrow' from Meyerhold and indeed seems not to have been impressed by any particular production of his." Yet later she observes that "If Meyerhold was ahead of his time, so that Brecht could have derived much from him, Brecht handed on in his own way certain Meyerholdian achievements now generally accepted without recognition of their source." *Meyerhold*, pp. 265–67.

1

BRECHT'S CONTACTS WITH THE THEATER OF MEYERHOLD

Vsevolod E. Meyerhold was born in Russia in 1874, the son of prosperous German parents. His career as a theatrical innovator began in 1903 and ended with his arrest in 1939. Well before the October Revolution, when Bertolt Brecht, the "Einstein of the new stage form," was still a boy, Meyerhold was known to St. Petersburg audiences as "the man with the new ideas."[1] Some of those ideas closely anticipated the theory and practice of Brecht. Most notable are those stylistic innovations used to destroy the realistic stage convention, such as film projections, posters which comment on or announce the action, interpolation of dances and songs, grotesque costuming, emphasis on stage movement and exaggerated gestures, abstract or highly simplified stage settings, and the training of actors as artistically and socially conscious performers. Beyond the fact that Brecht and Meyerhold were conditioned by the same revolutionary milieu, believed in a non-illusionistic art which serves humanity, and were attracted to similar elements in the traditional theaters of the Orient and the West, there were important historical connections which can illuminate any comparison of their dramatic theory and practice.

In "The Golden Twenties" and early 1930s Western artists and intellectuals showed considerable interest in the Soviet Union and the Bolshevik experiment. Their interest, if not always their political sympathies, was shared by the large number of Russians living abroad, a number growing rapidly due to the flood of new emigrés. The main target of this new migration was Berlin, already by the turn of the century the largest "Russian" city outside Russia. Carl Zuckmayer has described the cultural atmosphere he and his friend Brecht enjoyed in the Berlin of the 1920s: aspiring young writers could sit around café tables with the likes of Eisenstein and Pudovkin, listening "worshipfully" to their talk and soaking up the "productive . . . stimulating" Russian ambience.[2]

Before the turn of the century Russians had come to Germany to sit at the feet of German university professors; after 1900, as Zuckmayer suggests, Russians increasingly brought to the West new ideas in the plastic arts, theater, literature, music, and the sciences. In his recently published memoir, Roman Jakobson claimed for Russian culture of the early twentieth century " 'a truly worldwide significance': it was not only imitating Western developments, but carrying them forward along original lines. Moreover, the Russians were beginning to think about these problems [of painting and poetry] theoretically to a much greater extent than their European counterparts, and to place them in a broad scientific-philosophical frame."[3]

The modern Russian Time of Troubles—First World War, the revolutions of 1917, and civil war—accelerated the flow of emigrants to Germany. By the end of 1919 approximately 70,000 Russians were living in Berlin and were arriving at a rate of more than 1,000 a month. They tended to settle in the southwestern section of the city, near the Tiergarten, gathering in cafés on the Nollendorfplatz and on the Kurfürstendamm to talk politics, philosophy, and art, and to listen to poetry readings. Viktor Shklovsky, Andrei Bely, and Vladimir Mayakovsky were among the writers who frequented the Russian cafés where German artists and intellectuals also liked to gather. There were dozens of such places, "with balalaikas, and zurnas, with gypsies, pancakes, shashlyk and, naturally, the inevitable heartbreak."[4] There were cabarets run by Russian emigrants, including Berlin's famous "Bluebird" whose performers made guest appearances throughout Germany. The performers wore Cubist costumes with wheel-like hats, cone-shaped sleeves, and cylindrical pants. In 1923 a correspondent for an American theater journal, reporting that "Berlin is now the second largest city of Russia," ecstatically described the brilliant explosion of avant-garde Russian-inspired Berlin theater.[5]

Interest among Germans and Russian emigrés for news about the Soviet Union was answered in part by German-Soviet friendship organizations such as the League of Friends of the Soviet Union, which was founded in 1928 and attracted mainly working-class people, and the Society of Friends of the New Russia. The Society, founded in 1923, drew primarily on artists and intelligentsia for its members; many of them, such as Hanns Eisler, Erwin Piscator, and Johannes R. Becher, knew Brecht well. The Society published the journal *Das neue Russland* (*New Russia*) and sponsored lectures by visiting Soviet cultural leaders. One of the visiting lecturers was Anatoly Lunacharsky, a lover of theater, the first Commissar of Enlightenment (1917–1929), a frequent contributor to *Das neue Russland*, and a friend of both Meyerhold and Brecht. Meyerhold's protégé Sergei Eisenstein spoke on Soviet film; an actor from Tairov's Kamerny Theater lectured on "The New Russian Theatrical Art"; Brecht's friend (and Meyerhold's colleague) Serge Tretiakov gave a report on "The Socialist Countryside and Its Writers." The Society's section for literature and art presented evenings of Russian music, readings of Russian literature, and screenings of Soviet films.[6]

In 1925 a special edition of *Das neue Russland*, devoted to theater (and especially Meyerhold's theater) in the Soviet Union, evoked additional articles and interviews about Soviet theater in other German journals and newspapers.[7] Among the Meyerhold productions which were reviewed in detail in *Das neue Russland* were *The Magnanimous Cuckold*, *The Earth Rampant*, *Trust D. E.*, *The Warrant*, *The Forest*, *Teacher Bubus*, and *Roar, China!* All these plays, as the reviewers pointed out, were extremely important as vehicles for Meyerhold's latest innovations. In 1926 the same journal reported that Meyerhold had visited Berlin Society members in order to entrust them with the arrangements for his ensemble's German tour.[8]

Besides *Das neue Russland*, a wide variety of periodical literature published in Berlin and other German cities regularly reported on Soviet cultural events, including Soviet theater. Some of these reports were quite detailed, such as those done in 1921 by Arthur Holitscher and Max Barthel on the revolutionary mass theatricals being produced in Petrograd. In 1922 articles on Meyerhold's work appeared in *Das literarische Echo* and *Der Gegner*. From 1924 the German revolutionary workers' press, particularly *Die rote Fahne* and *AIZ* (*Arbeiter-Illustrierte Zeitung*) reported frequently on Soviet theater.[9] In 1926 the prestigious political journal *Die Weltbühne* published a detailed essay on Meyerhold's innovations, praising his revitalization of the techniques of *commedia dell' arte*, with its masks, improvisations, and consciously "theatrical" theater. The article also described Meyerhold's Eastern-style presentation of Blok's *The Fairground Booth*, with its narrating "author," simply dressed "stage hands" who openly carried on and removed props, and uncurtained stage. In addition there was a description of Meyerhold's efforts to advance stage decoration into a full-blown art for the theater: "not a painted theater, but a theatricalization of painting."[10]

In 1928 Brecht's friend and associate Bernhard Reich (formerly a director with the *Deutsches Theater* in Berlin and the Munich *Kammerspiele*), who had emigrated to the Soviet Union, published an article in *Die literarische Welt* in which he expressed approval of Meyerhold's episodic, gestic style, a style which "already embodies the sort of revue theater which is Bert Brecht's unrealized dream."[11] In the same year *Scene* (Berlin) carried an essay on Meyerhold's innovations. The author, Bess Brenck-Kalischer, had just returned from Moscow; she had attended rehearsals at the Meyerhold Theater and seen productions of *The Forest* and *Roar, China!* Articles such as these and information brought from Russia by friends helped Brecht keep up with Soviet theater.[12]

Russian ensembles became fairly commonplace in Germany after 1906, the year Stanislavsky's Moscow Art Theater made its first German tour. From then until the early 1930s, except for the war years, Russian and Soviet companies were warmly received and evoked a great deal of critical discussion. The third of August 1923 marked the beginning of a series of visits by avant-garde Soviet directors and their troupes. From the third to the ninth the Vakhtangov Theater was in Berlin, playing to full houses each night. Tairov's *Kamerny* Theater also turned up in Germany late that year, performing in Berlin and other cities.

A theatrical exhibition held in Magdeburg (May-June 1927) included the *Kamerny* (in the otherwise all-German presentation)
as an ensemble "which had exerted a great influence on the
development of modern German theater."[13]

In 1927 German audiences were entertained by a Soviet agitprop group known as Blue Blouse, the direct descendant of
Russian political avant-garde theater. The influence of Blue Blouse
on German political ensemble theater was profound.[14] In Berlin
the troupe performed at Piscator's theater where Brecht worked
as a writer. Among Brecht's papers is a 1928 article on Blue
Blouse theater by Harry Wilder of the Berlin Proletarian Experimental Theater. Sections of the essay describing the organization of Blue Blouse theater in Germany and the Soviet Union
have been bracketed and underlined. The way the rest of the
essay is marked and annotated indicates that the reader was
especially interested in Wilder's observation that Soviet Blue
Blouse texts were not very useful to Germany because of differing political conditions. Nevertheless, Wilder pointed out,
German Blue Blouse troupes could exploit Soviet techniques,
especially the sparing use of props, with the actor's body the
main prop. The conclusion of Wilder's article must have held
particular interest for Brecht: "They [the Soviet Blue Blouse
troupes] have actualized what for us has been a theoretical challenge" (*Sie haben praktisch verwirklicht, was bei uns theoretisch als
Forderung bestand*).[15]

In the spring of 1930, Meyerhold brought his ensemble to
Germany for their first foreign tour. Brecht evidently saw at least
one of the performances (Tretiakov's *Roar, China!*) because he
defended it against the attacks of conservative critics. Brecht was
upset by German reviews of the Meyerhold productions and
thought German critics did not appreciate Meyerhold's contribution to the theory and practice of rational socio-political theater. Of all the plays presented by the Meyerhold troupe, Brecht
guessed that *Roar, China!* was the most irritating to conservative
sensibilities. The reviewers had faulted Meyerhold and Tretiakov
for presenting a lopsided view of colonialist savagery, a criticism
Brecht thought ridiculous.[16] In fact, Tretiakov's play turned out
to be one of the most popular productions in the Meyerhold
repertoire and was soon produced all over the world, from New

York (by the Theatre Guild in 1930, under the direction of Herbert Biberman, who had spent several months in the Soviet Union) to Japan. The drama (which premiered in Moscow in 1926) was based on a bloody incident that occurred in China during the author's stay there in 1924.[17]

One of the leading roles in the play, that of an Old Boatman who volunteers to be executed in order to save the lives of others, was enacted by Nikolai Okhlopkov, then Meyerhold's student. As a director of various avant-garde theaters he was to become a most effective continuer of his teacher's ideas, as well as an innovator in his own right. Tretiakov introduced Brecht to Okhlopkov when Brecht went to Moscow in 1935. At that time Brecht saw Okhlopkov's production of *Aristocrats* and *The Start*, performances which utilized theatrical devices pioneered or planned by Meyerhold: a stage platform in the midst of the audience, and stage assistants in black tights and masks who showered the stage and audience with a "snowstorm" of white confetti. (The black-clad stage attendants who openly manufacture theatrical effects are a device of Kabuki theater which Meyerhold had used at least as early as 1914.) Brecht also saw Michoels' *King Lear* at the Jewish Theater. When Brecht made his last visit to Moscow in 1955, he urged Okhlopkov to revive *Aristocrats*.[18]

During the six weeks the Meyerhold group toured Germany, hundreds of reviews and articles about them appeared in the German press. People were struck by Meyerhold's use of mass scenes in which numbers of ordinary working people took part, as in the performance of *Roar, China!* and Selvinsky's *The Second Army Commander* (1929). Doubtless they were also impressed when his actors, in their turn, participated in a May Day demonstration in Cologne. This was very much in harmony with Meyerhold's belief that actors should be intellectually and politically aware, onstage or off.[19]

Kamerny Theater, Vakhtangov Theater, Blue Blouse, and the Meyerhold troupe exemplify the relatively free passage of dramatic art from Russia to the West. Among the important individual transmitters were Anna Lacis, Bernhard Reich, Anatoly Lunacharsky, Sergei Tretiakov, and Sergei Eisenstein. German artists and intellectuals (such as Brecht, Piscator, Ernst Toller, Johannes R. Becher, Hugo Huppert, and Walter Benjamin) in their turn travelled to the Soviet Union to experience for themselves the tenor of art and life in what was heralded as a new and more humane society. Brecht made four trips to that part of the world (1932, 1935, 1941, and 1955). For Hugo Huppert, a Viennese poet and Mayakovsky scholar who lived in the Soviet Union during the 1920s, those were "holy years" of contact with brilliant men and women.[20]

These personal contacts provided a source of new ideas for Brecht and granted him vivid access to Meyerhold's innovations. For example, when Brecht travelled to the Soviet Union in 1932, for the first showing of the film *Kuhle Wampe* (screenplay by Brecht, music by Hanns Eisler), he was accompanied by the film's director, Slatan Dudow, a Bulgarian who had emigrated to Berlin in 1922. During 1925–26, while studying at the University of Berlin Theater Institute under Max Hermann, Dudow got practical theater experience with Leopold Jessner and Jürgen Fehling. From September 1927 to June 1928 Dudow worked under Piscator. At Hermann's request Dudow went to Moscow in April 1929 to collect material for his research on Soviet theater. In Moscow he attended showings at the Meyerhold Theater, as well as at the Bolshoi Theater, the Moscow Art Theater, and the theaters of Tairov and Vakhtangov. He also met Eisenstein, who was in the company of Mayakovsky and Tretiakov. Probably because of that meeting, Dudow returned to Berlin in the autumn of 1929 with instructions to speak to Brecht about a Russian translation of *Drums in the Night*. It was also about this time, perhaps as a result of his talks with Brecht, that Dudow wrote to Mayakovsky indicating that "certain people" were interested in producing Mayakovsky's *The Bedbug* (directed by Meyerhold, 1929) on the German stage. In November 1929 the Schiffbauerdamm people sent a letter to Festland Publishers stating that they were already well acquainted with the text of *The Bedbug* and were "extraordinarily interested" in producing it. The theater inquired whether Festland could give them official permission to produce the play and provide them with copies of the music. Although *The Bedbug* project was never realized, Brecht and Dudow began a long collaboration. Besides the one film, they worked together, from 1930 to 1938, on six of Brecht's plays.[21]

Another of Brecht's important contacts with Russian theater and Meyerhold was the Latvian Anna Lacis (1891–1979). Her father was a factory worker who managed to send his daughter to a private *Gymnasium* in Riga, where several outstanding Latvian artists taught. In 1913 Lacis moved to St. Petersburg and enrolled in the famous Psychoneurological Institute, founded and headed by the pioneer psychologist V. M. Bekhterev (1857–1927), a brilliant educator-scientist who had a special interest in child rearing and early education.[22]

In St. Petersburg Lacis saw a number of productions of the Imperial theaters, then under Meyerhold's directorship. In her memoirs she describes his theatrical experiments. His production of Sologub's *The Hostages of Life* (1913) had the proscenium "covered with blue material. On the stage were an endless succession of doors, through which the actors entered, exited, appeared, vanished, like a many-colored conveyor belt—a symbol of the absurd chaos of life." In Pinero's *Mid-Channel* (1914) the stage was constructed entirely of cubes, to the great scandal of Petersburg. Even the actors balked at performing. One critic wrote that Meyerhold had turned the academic theater into a "futuristic Hanswurstiade." Lacis also saw some of Meyerhold's early and important innovative work with opera. He was fascinated by the possible uses of music and dance in every sort of theatrical production. His presentation in 1913 of Strauss's *Electra* also provoked fierce critical attacks, though some reviewers saw this work as progressive music-drama. "We students," wrote Lacis, "were on their side."[23]

In addition to performances and reviews, Lacis could read about Meyerhold's experimental theater in the journal *The Love of Three Oranges*. Meyerhold was the editor and a frequent contributor to the publication, which chronicled his studio's activities and also included various articles on dramatic theory and the history of theater.[24] Even when Lacis left the capital for Moscow in 1914 to study under Fedor Komissarzhevskii, her links with Meyerhold's ideas continued to be strengthened, for Komissarzhevskii had worked with Meyerhold and in many respects had assimilated his dramatic theory and practice.[25]

Lacis was especially interested in Meyerhold's experiments with the dramatic use of movement and, judging by her memoirs, tremendously impressed by "Theater October," an idea which the director launched in 1920. Its purpose was to combine agitational and propagandistic drama with new theatrical forms. Meyerhold himself acted as commander, donned a Red Army uniform, and went out both to meet with workers, soldiers, and peasants and to organize them into theatrical groups. Later Lacis would acknowledge that her own work as director and theater critic "owes much to Meyerhold."[26]

The theatrical experience which Lacis eventually brought to Germany included not only her knowledge of Meyerhold's work and the work of other avant-garde Russians, but her own rich experience in children's theater and the study of reflexology under Bekhterev. At first she worked in Orel, concentrating on children in state orphanages, devising theatrical activities for them as a means of reviving their interest in life. Later, perhaps inspired by her teacher (who "ardently participated in the reform of the homeless children"), she tried to help the often brutalized child gangs that roamed Russia, victims of war, revolution, and civil war.[27] Reiner Steinweg has suggested connections between Lacis' studies under Bekhterev, her children's theater, her friendship with Brecht and Walter Benjamin (the latter wrote a theoretical analysis of her work in children's theater),[28] and Brecht's theory of didactic theater. Steinweg points out that Brecht's didactic plays tend to be directed toward children and/or written to be performed by schoolchildren with their choruses and orchestras, and traces the possible influence of Lacis on Brecht's *Lehrstücktheorie* ultimately to her study in Bekhterev's Institute.[29] Lacis tried to teach children to be acute observers of the world around them, and in order to develop their ability to listen and see (Brecht's "art of observation"), her theater included workshops in music and art. The section for painting and sketching was taught by Victor Chestakov, who later became a set designer for Meyerhold.[30]

In 1922 Lacis went to Berlin where she met the director Bernhard Reich, then with the *Deutsches Theater*; he would be her life's companion. The following year she and Reich travelled to Munich where Reich had been appointed Chief Director of the Munich *Kammerspiele*. It was in Munich that Lacis and Reich met Brecht, also a *Kammerspiele* director; he had just begun to plan

the production of his and Feuchtwanger's play *The Life of Edward
II of England*.[31] When Brecht was introduced to Lacis he ques-
tioned her about the Russian theater, the Soviet Union, and
Soviet art policy.[32] He offered her the job of production assistant
and in addition the role of young Edward.[33]

During rehearsals Brecht tried to perfect the dramatic movement of the actors. According to Lacis, "He wanted every gesture
to express the whole character: he formed dialogue and verse
differently from what the actors were accustomed to. He wanted
them to avoid whatever was vague, foggy, common. That was
the beginning of *gestic* speech."[34] Lacis did not draw any parallels
between Brecht's development of gestic expression and similar
work done by Meyerhold. Yet, at the very time when she had
been introduced to his theater in 1913, the Russian director was
teaching his students the art of gesture and writing about the
"scenario of movement" in various brochures which were passed
around among his students. "Movement," he wrote at that time,

"is the most powerful means of theatrical expression."[35]

Lacis met Walter Benjamin in May 1924, and later that year,
in Berlin, she introduced him to Brecht. It was mainly on account
of his love for her that Benjamin travelled to the Soviet Union
in 1925 and 1926. During his two months in Moscow (December
1926–February 1927) Benjamin attended several theaters, but was
impressed only with Meyerhold's productions. Because both
Reich and Lacis knew Meyerhold, Benjamin was able to get
tickets to *The Inspector General*, *The Forest*, and *Trust D. E.* During
the first intermission of *Trust D. E.* Lacis introduced Benjamin
to Meyerhold, who promptly arranged a private guided tour
through the Meyerhold Theater Museum. In his diary Benjamin
recorded that he and Lacis saw the models for Meyerhold's stage
settings, including the "first-rate setting for *Cocu magnifique*, the
famous scenery from *Bubus* with its bamboo frame (the canes
accompany the actors' entrances and exits as well as all the
important moments of the play with loud or soft chimes), the
bow of the ship from *Roar, China!* with water on the forestage
and other things."[36]

The Inspector General was the most important production which
Reich, Lacis, and Benjamin saw that year. Meyerhold's adaptation and staging of Gogol's classic provoked more controversy

than was customary even for Meyerhold's innovations. The Soviet critics protested his tampering with a national treasure. Meyerhold, however, had always asserted the director's right to alter a text, and with *The Inspector General* he freely used that right: he added dialogue, characters, and scenes from other of Gogol's works, and rejected the traditional interpretation of the play as sheer farce by presenting it as a pessimistic vision of public and private vanity, stupidity, and hypocrisy. In order to defend his ideas, Meyerhold organized a public debate about his version of the play. Reich, Lacis, and Benjamin attended the discussion and the latter two wrote about it—Lacis decades later but Benjamin shortly after the event. There was more at stake than the question of his artistic franchise, for Meyerhold, despite his fame and influence, was having difficulties with the official criticism. Though the roster of speakers was heavily weighted in Meyerhold's behalf (the speakers included Mayakovsky and Lunacharsky), Benjamin guessed that this debate signalled the beginning of a deathblow for Meyerhold: "The party and the press have rejected Meyerhold's work. . . . His opponents won out completely. . . . Neither Lunacharsky nor Mayakovsky could save him. . . . From now on there is an anti-Meyerhold front."[37]

Lacis returned to Germany in the early fall of 1928 as an official consultant from the film department of the Commissariat of Enlightenment to the Soviet trade mission in Berlin, and emissary from the Soviet Proletarian Theater to the German Union of Proletarian-Revolutionary Writers (BPRS: *Bund proletarisch-revolutionärer Schriftsteller*). Under sponsorship of BPRS she gave public lectures on the most notable playwrights and directors then at work in the Soviet Union. She frequently met with "the three Bs"—Brecht, Benjamin, and Becher—and discussed Soviet theater. They often talked about Sergei Tretiakov, who was a close associate of Meyerhold and became a good friend of Brecht.[38]

Tretiakov, like Lacis, was born in Latvia and educated in Riga. During the Civil War he first fought with the Whites, but later joined the Bolsheviks, for whom he became a devoted worker, both as government official and as artist. From the early twenties he was in the thick of the Futurist movement, collaborating with Mayakovsky as editor of, and contributor to the Futurist journals *LEF* and (its successor) *Novyi LEF* (*Left* and *New Left*). A tireless political evangelist, traveller, and social activist, Tretiakov turned his experiences (in China, for example, or on a collective farm in the Caucasus) into popular literature, much of which was published in Weimar Germany. Brecht first met Tretiakov in Germany in the late twenties or early thirties, and soon the two men became close friends. When, in 1932, Brecht and Dudow travelled to Moscow for the premiere of *Kuhle Wampe*, Tretiakov was their cicerone.

In my friendship with Brecht, I have experienced that feeling of com-
radely closeness which makes one strong. I translate his work; I accept
much of it, I protest much of it, but I follow his every step with the
utmost attention, if you will, with love. Just such relationships, just
such an exchange of letters, I wish for each of you.

> (From a speech by Tretiakov to the First All-Union
> Congress of Soviet Writers, June 1934.).[39]

In a poem mourning Tretiakov's violent death (condemned as a spy by a People's Court, he was shot in 1939 in a Siberian concentration camp), Brecht calls him "My teacher." The poem is entitled "Is the People Infallible?" and in each stanza the poet asks, "Suppose he is innocent?"[40]

Tretiakov's association with Meyerhold began in 1922. The former had just returned from the Far East, and the latter was beginning his own theater and actors' studio. Tretiakov became deeply involved in those enterprises as administrator, organizer, and playwright. The two men complemented each other artist-ically: Tretiakov, a "master of dramatic language," and Meyer-hold, who at that very time was formulating his theory of biomechanics and working on the problem of including "verbal elements in the exercises of dramatic movement." Together they started a course called "word-movement." Evidently Tretiakov had a lot to do with developing the theory and practice of bio-mechanics, as Meyerhold himself testified, and "more than any-one else" helped create a theoretical underpinning for the work of the Meyerhold Theater.[41]

In 1933 during an informal meeting of writers at the offices of *Literaturnaia gazeta* (one of the Soviet Union's foremost literary magazines) Tretiakov argued that a play should not only be relevant to current social problems but also offer a "prognosis" of future political and social conditions. He offered as example his own *Roar, China!* He also told the writers that he had translated and reworked three of Brecht's plays "to the extent that they differ fundamentally from the author's originals." These adaptations were published the following year.[42] A few years later, in his turn, Brecht adapted a German version of Tretiakov's play *I Want a Baby*.[43]

Tretiakov: The playgoer is not finally satisfied—[with Brecht's problematic theater] this is what troubles Brecht. The playgoer leaves anxious . . .

Usovsky: A perplexed playgoer?

Tretiakov: No. A thinking playgoer.

Amaglobeles: Isn't the playgoer a thinking one to Sophocles?

Tretiakov: The problem of the playwright is to lift the playgoer out of his equilibrium so that he will not leave serene but ready for action.[44]

Tretiakov's observation about the "thinking playgoer" complements an anecdote Walter Benjamin told of Meyerhold:

The Russian producer Meyerhold was recently [1930] asked in Berlin what in his opinion distinguished his actors from those of Western Europe. He replied: "Two things. First, they think; second, they do not think idealistically but materialistically." . . . The epic actor is oriented towards knowledge, and this knowledge, in turn, determines not only the content but also the tempo, pauses, and stresses of his whole performance.[45]

When Brecht travelled to Russia a second time in 1935, he and his wife, the actress Helene Weigel, stayed in the Tretiakovs' Moscow apartment. It was there, during a discussion of theatrical matters, that Reich first heard the word *Verfremdung*:

We spoke about a very unusual theatrical performance. . . . I referred to a certain detail of the production [Okhlopkov's staging of Pogodin's *Aristocrats*] and Tretiakov interjected: "Yes, that's a *Verfremdung*," and darted a conspiratorial glance at Brecht. Brecht nodded. That was my first acquaintance with the word *Verfremdung*. So I must assume that

Brecht got this term from Tretiakov; I think that Tretiakov somewhat recast Shklovsky's term *otchuzhdenie*, "to distance,"[46] "to alienate."[47]

Critics have debated the proposition that Brecht's V-Effect derives from the theories of Russian Formalism. John Willett argues that it comes directly from the writings of Victor Shklovsky, the leading Formalist.[48] Others object, namely Soviet and DDR critics (Formalism has been out of favor in the Soviet Union since about 1930) and some Western writers because of insufficient evidence or on linguistic grounds.[49] Jan Knopf claims there is no evidence that Brecht met with any Russian Formalist while in Moscow in 1935 and that in any case, the Formalists were not interested in non-esthetic problems. This argument ignores the close ties between Futurists and Formalists, a relationship which is clearly shown in Shklovsky's memoir *Mayakovsky and His Circle*, as well as by a reading of any of the numbers of *LEF* and *Novyi LEF*, journals of avant-garde literature and art which were produced by people who called themselves Futurists or Formalists or both, such as Shklovsky, Tretiakov, Mayakovsky, Brik, Terentev. In Tretiakov, Brecht had a friend who was at the very center of the Futurist-Formalist movement. In any case, by 1928 none of the Formalists believed that literature must be studied apart from anything else.[50]

On an April evening in 1935, Brecht, by then a refugee with no permanent home, was the guest of honor at a Moscow gathering of Russian and German intellectuals and artists, a meeting sponsored by the Writers' Union. Tretiakov spoke on Brecht's "epic" theater and on his artistic and political significance. Kirsanov read his translation of Brecht's "Legend of the Dead Soldier" and actors from the *Kamerny* Theater performed excerpts from *The Threepenny Opera*. Wieland Herzfelde spoke on Brecht's role in German poetry, and Lacis gave her views of him as a director. The highlight of the evening was Carola Neher singing ballads from *The Threepenny Opera*. Brecht must have pleased his Russian hosts (and helped keep a vital escape route open) when he declared that there was only one significant city for theater in all the world: Moscow.[51]

During this same visit Brecht, along with Meyerhold, Tretiakov, Eisenstein, and others, saw performances of the Chinese

actor Mei Lan-fang and his troupe. If Brecht found in the Formalist theories of Shklovsky certain ideas which complemented
or even inspired his own, he saw in the centuries-old yet innovative art of Mei the very embodiment of those ideas. In
particular Brecht admired the ability of the Chinese actor to
separate himself emotionally from his role so that the audience
was never tempted to forget that acting and not everyday life
was occurring onstage. Human gestures and everyday speech
were transformed by the actors into art.[52] Brecht found the mental attitude demanded of a Chinese theater audience very much
to his liking. In order to enjoy their national drama fully, the
Chinese must attend the theater armed with a working knowledge of its rules. Thus the playgoers have their own special skills
which they bring to the play. Moreover, these skills are not
limited to a select group of intellectuals but are the accomplish-
ment of an entire people. The Moscow performance of Mei Lan-
fang realized for Brecht his idea of a non-illusionistic drama
which attracted a mass audience of ordinary people who neither
wished nor expected to be hypnotized by the actors.[53]

Mei's repertoire included the stock female roles of Chinese
theater: the good-hearted matron, the aged woman, the loose
housemaid, the woman warrior. Eisenstein liked Mei's woman
warrior best. In this role Mei accomplished a sort of double
alienation by impersonating a woman who impersonates a man.
It may be that this performance, together with Tretiakov's interest in and experience of Chinese culture (as reflected in *Roar,
China!* and his 1930 novel *Den Shi-hua*), provided Brecht with
certain ideas which bore fruit in *The Good Person of Sezuan* for
which Brecht created a female-male central character.

Meyerhold was also taken by the performance of the Chinese
actors, so much so that he dedicated to Mei his next production,
Griboedov's *Woe to Wit*, in which he incorporated "features from
the theatrical 'folklore' of the Chinese troupe."[54] At a public
discussion about the troupe's performances[55] Meyerhold spoke
on various aspects of Mei's art, in particular the use of gesture
and rhythmical movement.[56]

It was a remarkable occurrence—the gathering of some of the
brightest leaders of the performing arts, including Brecht, Meyerhold, and Eisenstein, to witness and openly discuss the ancient

art of Chinese theater as performed by a great master crafts-
man—especially in 1935 in Moscow under the auspices of a
massively and murderously repressive regime. There is no evidence that Brecht and Meyerhold directly exchanged ideas on
this occasion, though Mei's performance, especially its theatricality and its innovative use of folk art, obviously touched on
theatrical principles which both men shared. It is quite possible
they met since Tretiakov, one of the chief organizers of the
gathering, was closely associated with Meyerhold and mainly
responsible for bringing Brecht to Moscow. As in the case of
Anna Lacis, Tretiakov is a likely transmitter of ideas between
the two directors.

In 1923 Tretiakov set down some Brechtian fundamentals about
theater. At the time, of course, he had not even heard of Brecht,
whose ideas on theater and whose directing career were only just
beginning to take shape. What Tretiakov had in mind were what
he considered to be Meyerhold's most important theatrical ideas:
the transformation of the traditional stage into agitprop theater,
of the "academic" actor into a socially active organizer of the
masses, of the audience from a "chance gathering" into a

firmly established collective which interacts with the play, the transfer
of attention from the purely narrative aspects of the play to the methods
of its construction, [and] the invention of the best methods for the
organization of a group into a cooperating collective.[57]

These ideas represent revolutionary changes in theatrical goals;
they are a part of the innovative approach to theater pioneered
by Tretiakov and Meyerhold and transmitted, perhaps, to Brecht.
Evidence of a Meyerhold-Tretiakov-Brecht connection can be
seen in Brecht's play *The Caucasian Chalk Circle*, with its rosy
picture of Soviet life.

The first part of that play, "The Conflict Over the Valley," is
set in the Caucasus during the time of reconstruction after World
War II and concerns a parcel of land claimed by two different
collective farms. One farm specializes in goat breeding; the other
cultivates fruit. The goatherds, who were obliged to abandon
their valley during the German occupation, wish to reclaim cus-

tody of the land. In the meantime, however, the fruit growers had moved in and designed an irrigation project to make the valley more bountiful. They think the prior claim of the goat breeders should be overruled by the circumstance that they, the fruit growers, will put the land to better use.

As the play begins, an official arbitrator from Moscow, known only as the Specialist, reads aloud the claims of both sides and then asks delegates from the two farms to debate the problem among themselves and attempt to resolve it. The goatherds are quickly persuaded that the fruit growers will make the best use of the land and so renounce their prior claim. The debate ends, and in the general rejoicing that follows a Singer comes onstage to entertain the farmers and the Specialist. As the Singer tells his story, which takes place in medieval Georgia but symbolically parallels the events just concluded, a group of farmers enacts it: A young maidservant named Grusche rescues the baby son of the governor when the boy's mother abandons him during the crisis of war. Grusche nurses the infant at great risk to her own safety and happiness. In the course of time, as the result again of the fortunes of war, the governor's wife (now a widow) returns to claim her son. She does not love the boy but needs him in order to acquire her late husband's fortune. On the other hand, Grusche has taken good care of the child, loves him, and does not want to surrender him. The two women bring their dispute before a judge named Azdak, a wily rascal of lowly origins, who finds himself, through the vicissitudes of war and social upheaval, elevated to the High Court of Justice of Grusinia. He it is who decides the child's fate by employing the device of the chalk circle—with a paradoxical twist. In the Chinese play *The History of the Chalk Circle* (Brecht's source for this episode) the woman who refuses to hurt the child by pulling it out of the circle is judged to be the biological mother, and therefore, the one who truly loves it. In *The Caucasian Chalk Circle* it is the adoptive mother who releases the child's arm. Azdak knows Grusche is not the "real" mother and therefore not legally entitled to the boy but nevertheless awards him to her. The play ends with the Singer's final verses which speak first of Azdak and his wonderful judgments and then conclude with a general commentary on the morality of ownership: everything, from wagons, to valleys, to children, ought to belong only to the most loving, the most capable, caretaker.

There are strong parallels, in theme and setting, between *The Caucasian Chalk Circle* and two German translations of works by Tretiakov: the play *I Want a Baby* and a book about collective farm life, *Field Marshals*.[58] *I Want a Baby* deals with the problem of who in a just society most deserves to raise children—the biological parents or some other agency? Which is better equipped to raise a child to make its contribution to the whole community? As in the *Chalk Circle*, this custody battle occurs against the background of life on a *kolkhoz* (collective farm).

Tretiakov's play concerns a young woman agronomist named Milda who decides to have a baby though she has neither husband nor lover (Tretiakov's choice of a name for his heroine is ironic; she is named after a Lithuanian love goddess). In choosing a child she will be guided by her idea of (political) eugenics. Her choice is a worker named Jakob. After quizzing him about his health, family background, and habits, she invites him to her room. Jakob is puzzled by the invitation but accepts. When he arrives at her room and she tells him her plan he is amazed but easily persuaded. After repeated visits by Jakob, Milda becomes pregnant, whereupon she abruptly dismisses him, much to his consternation, for he has become genuinely fond of Milda and knowledge of her pregnancy awakens in him strong paternal feelings. He wants to possess his child. Such irrational feelings are no part of Milda's plan, however. To her mind, the baby growing in her body, conceived according to her plan, belongs solely to her, to raise as she sees fit.

When the child is born she gives it to the farm nursery to be reared communally. She visits her son but never lets him know that she is his mother. At the end there is an emotional scene in which Jakob (now married and the father of other children) and Milda meet at the nursery. Time has passed, but Jakob still yearns for the child he has never met. He demands that Milda give the boy to him and his wife to raise or at least tell him which of the children in the nursery is his so that he can visit his son and show his love. Milda refuses Jakob's requests on the principle that one should love all children, not just one's own. At this impasse the play ends. There is no happy or right ending, as in *The Caucasian Chalk Circle*.

Milda's unquenchable desire for motherhood anticipated and perhaps is reflected in Grusche's devotion to her adopted child, as well as Kattrin's destruction because of her love for all children (in *Mother Courage*, 1941). In addition, Fritz Mierau has pointed out the similarity between Scene 9 of *I Want a Baby*, in which the father-to-be lovingly introduces his future child to everyday life ("Do you see the crows sitting on the telegraph wires? . . . Policeman, stop the traffic for us!") and the scene in Brecht's *The Good Person of Sezuan* in which Shen Te fondly shows her unborn child the world ("Here, this is a tree. . . . Oh, a policeman! We'll bow to him"). Brecht began writing *The Good Person of Sezuan* in 1930, about the time he received Tretiakov's play.

When Tretiakov presented his play to the Meyerhold Theater in 1926, he hoped to have it staged as a "dialectic drama" (a catchword which, from the 1930s, would become prominent in Brecht's writing),[59] wherein would be revealed social problems but not their solutions, thus forcing the playgoer to wrestle with these problems not only during the play but afterwards as well. In 1929 Tretiakov described the dialectic construction of *I Want a Baby* by comparing the stage to a trampoline or springboard from which the play takes off, unwinding in a spiral which reaches into the audience's discussions and into their non-theatrical lives.[60]

The second of Tretiakov's works which may have helped shape *The Caucasian Chalk Circle* is a book which grew out of the author's belief that artists need to have a practical understanding of the society in which they live, that in order to achieve this insight they must be active producers, as well as consumers, of its benefits. Prompted by these convictions, Tretiakov left Moscow in 1928 to live and work on a collective farm in the northern Caucasus. His experiences there were recreated in *Field Marshals*. According to Walter Benjamin, the book exercised a "crucial influence on the further organization of the collective farm economy."[61]

The nameless first person narrator of *Field Marshals* (presumably Tretiakov himself) parallels the Specialist of *The Caucasian Chalk Circle* and in some ways is like Judge Azdak. Tretiakov's

narrator is himself a specialist, a troubleshooter who comes from
Moscow, in part to act as arbitrator between disputing collective
farm workers. But also like Azdak he finds himself intervening
in private family quarrels. The problem of the best management
of both land and children is one of his main concerns; it is his
mission to convince the peasants that their traditional notions
of land and child "ownership" are not appropriate to the new
social order.

I held mass meetings in the collective farms and collected money for
the tractors and for the state fund. I explained Jakovlev's thesis (Jakovlev
is the people's Commissar of Agriculture). . . . I persuaded private farmers to join the collective. I made peace among quarreling mothers in
the nursery. I advised on distribution of the harvest. I investigated the
farmers' complaints from every aspect, in order to set things right.

(*Field Marshals*, 20)

The same conventions which demand private ownership of
land and livestock go hand-in-glove with the conviction that a
biological mother must raise her own child, regardless of her
child-rearing capabilities. The peasant women's stubborn re-
sistance to relinquishing their small plots and skinny cattle and
horses is surpassed only by their unwillingness to hand their
children over to the state nursery. Or, as one of the farmers
remarks: "The women who have their own farms take horses
from the kolkhoz's fields, and the collective farm wives steal
their children from the nurseries" (*Field Marshals*, 259). But in
the end (under the pressure of heavy field work) the women
finally come around to the idea of the communal nursery as a
necessary element of collective life.

In *Field Marshals* one episode especially anticipates the first
part of *The Caucasian Chalk Circle*. Here the narrator explains that
the *kolkhozniks* were accustomed to assemble in order to thrash
out disagreements having to do with farm operations. On one
such occasion the farmers find themselves divided into opposing
groups, the "new" and the "old" collectivists: those who live
on land recently annexed by the collective system, and those
who live on one of the older communes. The argument, over

whose fields are to be harvested first, gets increasingly hostile. "What do you think might happen after such a quarrel?" (Tretiakov asks the reader), "Fist fighting? Shouting?" Suddenly a voice of reason and reconciliation breaks through the emotionally charged atmosphere: "What's all this 'old' and 'new' stuff! We're all new here!" (*Field Marshals*, 365). Whereupon the assembled farmers, laying aside their division, proceed to tackle their problems as one community of workers. In this scene, as in *The Caucasian Chalk Circle*, it is not the government official but the people themselves who settle their dispute, according to the demands of the common good, rather than according to the dictates of violence and greed.

The first part of Brecht's play is sometimes regarded, by both critics and directors, as a superfluous appendage to an otherwise magnificent play, while the thematic relationship between the two sections (the fight over the valley and the fight over the child) is often downgraded as tenuous and artificial, "the non-Russian Stalinist's view of Stalin's Russia."[62] On the contrary, the hopeful vision of communal farm life that Brecht presents reflects what Tretiakov reported. Tretiakov planned but never completed a play based on *Field Marshals*, to be called *We Feed the Earth*. Brecht was quite interested in the play and urged his friend to finish it. In view of Brecht's interest in *I Want a Baby* as well as *We Feed the Earth*, it is probable that the two discussed the issues raised in these works, issues which were again exposed in *The Caucasian Chalk Circle*. Tretiakov may have been blind to the horrid realities of forced collectivization, but he was not simply a utopian visionary. *Field Marshals* shows the failures and frustrations as well as the successes of his communal work. True to his convictions about the responsibility of art and artists, he participated—vigorously and positively—in the social experiments of the 1920s and early 1930s. He seems not to have sensed the abyss just ahead, but his vision remains a cut above the usual socialist-realist *kitsch*.

Brecht wrote the first part of *The Caucasian Chalk Circle* in 1944 and located it geographically and temporally in post–World War II Russia during reconstruction. But the *kolkhoz* scene, like the Azdak story, is a flashback—it reflects a "golden time" when idealists such as Tretiakov could still believe in and work for the creation of a new socialist society, in which both land and children would be nurtured by those best qualified to care for them.

The dissemination of new ideas in the arts by cultural ambassadors such as Tretiakov was made possible in the 1920s partly because the official head of Soviet culture was Anatoly V. Lunacharsky (1875–1933), who also represents a link between Brecht and Soviet theater. Lunacharsky was the first Soviet Commissar of Enlightenment (1917–1929) and a man of vast culture and creative energy. He appeared to his contemporaries as "a man in a 'smoking jacket,' pointed graying goatee, inquisitive, intently scrutinizing, narrowed eyes."[63] The commissar joined the Russian Social Democratic Party in 1897 and worked with Lenin on pre-revolutionary Bolshevik journals after 1904. From 1925 to the first half of 1931 he was a member of the editorial board of *Novyi Mir*. His approach to art was generally tolerant and eclectic; he never advocated or practiced the forceful suppression of politically unpopular ideas or art forms. As Commissar of Enlightenment, he encouraged the free play of conflicting ideas and often used his influence to get controversial art works past official censorship. Although he strove to protect and preserve Russia's artistic heritage, he also supported Proletkult, the (officially disfavored) arts organization whose leaders insisted on a complete break with their esthetic past, on freedom from any sort of political or governmental regulation, and whose style was strongly influenced by Meyerhold's avant-garde productions. Besides supporting experimentation in the arts, Lunacharsky came to the aid of artists who were starving or had been officially ostracized.[64]

Late in 1917 he invited 120 leading Russian artists to a conference to consider the problem of organizing the arts under state control. Meyerhold's decision to attend (only five accepted the invitation) "amounted to a hazardous act of faith," which he affirmed the next year by joining the Bolsheviks.[65] Soon after the arts conference Lunacharsky appointed Meyerhold a deputy chief (for Petrograd), and then in 1919 chief, of the Theatrical Department of the Commissariat of Enlightenment. The two men remained on a good personal footing despite sharp ideological differences which were occasioned by Meyerhold's zealous attacks on traditional art forms.[66] It is to the commissar's great credit that he worked for the peaceful co-existence of the old and the new in art by protecting traditional forms from the onslaughts of enthusiastic revolutionaries like Meyerhold, and by protecting innovators from reactionaries.

Before 1917, when Meyerhold's work was avant-garde but apolitical, Lunacharsky complained that the former's "bourgeois instinct" and "decadent sentiment" overpowered him.[67] But once Meyerhold had joined the Bolsheviks, Lunacharsky heartily welcomed him albeit with certain "ideological" reservations. Though he disapproved of Meyerhold's "leftist" excesses, he had nothing but praise for his theatrical genius. Moreover, he was convinced that Meyerhold was evolving a politically mature, socially useful, innovative, and uniquely Soviet contribution to the theater. He further believed that the director's use of music, dance, masks, circus devices, and the like helped extend the horizons of realism in the theater.[68] For the commissar's idea of "realism" was not a narrow concept tightly bound to certain conventions of nineteenth-century art. Rather, Lunacharsky held a view of realism very similar to Brecht's and Meyerhold's in that he welcomed the use of any device or style which could promote an awareness of the world as it is and as it may become. He seemed to regard Meyerhold as a living embodiment of the principle that better forms will inevitably emerge if opposing ideas are given the opportunity to develop and conflict. To those who condemned Meyerhold's production of *The Inspector General*, Lunacharsky wrote, "of course, there will continue to be arguments about *The Inspector General*. So what!? Let's argue!"[69]

Lunacharskaia-Rozenel recounts a meeting between her husband and Brecht in 1928 at the Schiffbauerdamm Theater, during a performance of *The Threepenny Opera* (they had previously met at gatherings of one of the Soviet-German friendship societies). After the performance the Lunacharskys were invited to join Brecht and various members of the cast along with Kurt Weill and several of Brecht's other friends and associates. Lunacharskaia recalls that the Germans pressed her husband for information on the latest plays being produced in the Soviet Union. They already knew *Teacher Bubus* (by A. Faiko) and *The Warrant* (by N. Erdman), both of which had been staged by Meyerhold in 1925. They asked Lunacharsky to recommend other Soviet plays, but he instead recommended that the theater of Brecht be introduced to Russia, and promised to speak to the directors Tairov and Radlov about producing *The Threepenny Opera* in Moscow and Leningrad.[70] In fact, Lunacharsky was eager to have the play staged in the Soviet Union. He envisioned an adaptation loosely based on Brecht and Gay—but no tampering with Weill's music!—which would make the play especially relevant for Soviet audiences. When the first Soviet version did appear in 1930, under Tairov's direction, "purely as entertainment drama," it disappointed both Lunacharsky and Brecht.[71]

In his 1928 review of the Berlin production, Lunacharsky remarked on the similarities between the devices used by Brecht and those employed by the Soviet theatrical organization TRAM (Young Workers' Theater):

Of course, the parallels are purely coincidental. The production of the *Opera* is extremely realistic . . . but just as in TRAM (which is also realistic), music suddenly bursts over the stage, people dance or sing. TRAM realism loves to suddenly shift into an interlude, to an imitation of film, to Expressionist fantasy. These elements are present in the Berlin production of *The Threepenny Opera*, in a lesser degree, perhaps, but in a very sophisticated style.[72]

Perhaps the resemblances between the two styles were not as coincidental as Lunacharsky presumed, given the contacts between Brecht and Soviet theater. The Leningrad TRAM, which was the most famous of the TRAM ensembles, "sprang from the womb of the Meyerhold system."[73] In her history of the German revolutionary theater, Anna Lacis emphasized the impact on German theater of TRAM and other Soviet acting groups which derived their style and purpose from Meyerhold's pioneering "Theater October." Although Lacis (in 1935) denied the direct influence of Meyerhold on either Piscator or Brecht, she pointed out that the Soviet Blue Blouse troupes made such a forceful appearance in Germany that "a 'Blue Blouse' manner of acting became widely established" there. TRAM's contribution to German theater, according to Lacis, came specifically in the areas of "original reworkings" of plays and the "report" genre.[74]

Early in 1933 the Lunacharskys were again in Berlin and were invited to a party at Brecht's apartment, where the guests naturally talked about Germany's increasingly ominous political situation. Someone suggested that emigration was the only practical answer. Lunacharsky, citing his own example as an Old Bolshevik, urged his German friends to keep fighting, to remain at the ideological barricades, whether in Germany or abroad.[75] The commissar died of a heart attack later that year in the south of France (he had been relieved of his position as Commissar of Enlightenment and appointed Ambassador to Spain, a post which tended to be a prelude to being purged).

Lunarcharskaia claims that Brecht visited Moscow in 1936 (1935?), in connection with his editorship of *Das Wort*,[76] met with her, and reminisced about old times, savoring the memory of her husband's prophecy of a "Brecht Theater."[77] But by 1935 things which the commissar had once encouraged, artistic experimentation and the free flow of ideas, were about to be extinguished in Russia as in Germany. Brecht himself had been in exile since 1933. Though still at the ideological barricades, he was unable to get his plays produced in any major theater.

Tretiakov was arrested in 1938, convicted by a people's tribunal of spying for Japan, and shot to death in a Siberian prison camp the following year. Meyerhold was arrested in 1939. Evidently he was sentenced on February 1, 1940, after a secret trial, to ten years' solitary confinement. The next day he was shot. Shortly after his arrest, Meyerhold's second wife, the actress Zinaida Raikh, was hideously stabbed to death in their apartment, quite possibly by government agents.[78]

Brecht visited the Soviet Union again in 1941 on his way to the United States. Of all the friends and acquaintances he had in Russia only Reich greeted him when he arrived in Moscow. Brecht knew that Lacis had been arrested and imprisoned and promised Reich he would use his influence with a Soviet diplomat to intercede on her behalf.[79] But she remained in prison for ten years, and Reich also was eventually imprisoned. Thus ended what Huppert had called "the holy years."

Lev Kopelev has noted that Brecht's visits to Moscow in the 1930s were "abundant with encounters and observations which for a long time after influenced Brecht and grew in his consciousness."[80] These encounters were the culmination of several years of contact with Soviet art. News about Soviet avant-garde theater, of which Meyerhold was the acknowledged master, was of special interest to Brecht. As I have pointed out, there were various links between Brecht and Meyerhold: published reviews and reports, and personal contacts with Soviet friends and Soviet theater, with Russian emigrés, and with German friends who had emigrated to or visited the Soviet Union. Lacis, Reich, Benjamin, and Lunacharsky were among those who shared Brecht's artistic and political interests and had seen and admired Meyerhold's work. Even the greatest artists owe much to their times and to concepts their predecessors have developed. It does not detract from Brecht's achievements to suppose that he incorporated into his work some of the original accomplishments of Meyerhold, thus keeping alive the ideas of the Russian director even after the man himself had been destroyed and his work and name suppressed.

Given the sense of community shared by Russian and German intellectuals during these "holy years," what were Brecht's and Meyerhold's attitudes toward each other's work? I have seen no direct evidence that the two men ever met, though there were good opportunities, when Brecht saw *Roar, China!* in Berlin in 1930, for example, or when both attended the performances of Mei Lan-fang in Moscow in 1935.

History does not record whether Meyerhold had any thoughts about Brecht, whereas Brecht's writings (published and unpublished) include several references to the Meyerhold Theater. The earliest and warmest note was written in 1930 on the occasion of the Meyerhold ensemble's tour in Berlin. As the official Soviet attitude toward Meyerhold grew colder and colder, so apparently did Brecht's public appreciation of him. What few compliments he did pay tended to be rather left-handed and concerned only with the formal aspects of Meyerhold's work. After 1930 Brecht never again wrote about Meyerhold's social theory of theater, though it is precisely that aspect of Meyerhold's art which, judging by Brecht's own pronouncements, would have held the greatest interest for him.

John Willett made some notes on a 1956 conversation with Brecht in which the latter mentioned that "He saw *Camelias, The*

Forest, Roar China and others in Moscow in the 1930s [and/or on the company's Berlin visit in spring 1930]: wonderful, aber nicht auf den Sinn gespielt [not played for the meaning]. Really expressionist. Meyerhold a great man: he was murdered of course." Brecht went on to tell Willett of his admiration for Vakhtangov, whom he felt "made most use of *Verfremdung*," and that he saw Vakhtangov's productions of *Princess Turandot* and *The Dybbuk*.[81]

In 1937 Brecht wrote to an editor of *Theatre Workshop* which had run articles describing Stanislavsky's work as the first wave of Russian theater. It was not so much what the articles said but what they failed to say that angered Brecht:

nothing about society, nothing about economy, and even the revolution hasn't occurred. That whole technique was around in Tsarist times. Meyerhold is just a late offshoot, a kind of tumor, and the revolutionary part of his work, the substance, isn't even mentioned. Agitprop and Tram don't exist, Okhlopkov doesn't exist. They [presumably the authors of the articles] are really unregenerate intellectuals, hardcore bourgeois.[82]

The letter does not tell us much about Brecht's own view of Meyerhold's work. And in his later writings as well, there is little to remind us of the strong support he gave the Russian director in 1930 against hostile German critics. By 1939, the year Meyerhold was arrested, Brecht was giving himself and Piscator credit for pioneering epic theater, allowing only that, as a precursor of his own achievements Meyerhold's work was flawed and formalistic. Thus did epic theater advance "artificiality into art."[83]

There is no recognition that the devices and techniques used by Piscator to create modern political theater: film; narrating chorus; treadmill, elevator, and "global" stages; moving sets as part of the action; the linking of stage and audience; and so on were employed by Meyerhold as much as a decade earlier.[84] And when Brecht discussed the genesis of gestic acting, he mentioned silent film and particularly Chaplin, but not Meyerhold's theory of "pre-acting" or the training of actors in "biomechanics," exercises intended to give the actor a greater range of physical expression.

While Brecht was informed about the accomplishments of Soviet theater, which he described in 1935 as the "most progressive . . . in the world," he admitted to no profound influences on his own work from that direction. For example, he noted that epic theater (which he claimed was born with the premiere of *Baal* in 1923) owed something to German workers' agitprop troupes but does not mention the Soviet TRAM and Blue Blouse ensembles which inspired them and perhaps also inspired his *Lehrstücke.*[85]

In 1939 he named Meyerhold, Stanislavsky, Vakhtangov, Okhlopkov, and others as contributors to modern theater. In particular he mentioned Vakhtangov's and Meyerhold's use of dance devices from Oriental theater, Contructivism, and methods of grouping actors onstage. That same year he enumerated elements of Meyerhold's method which he felt were progressive: "opposition to the personal," "emphasis on the artistic," "mechanics of movement," and "abstract milieu." But where is mention of Meyerhold's development away from a completely nonrepresentative setting toward that fine mixture of the abstract and the realistic which was the hallmark of Brecht's own style?[86]

The Meyerhold Theater was closed in 1938. On that occasion an article appeared in the Moscow journal *Das Wort* which attempted to explain why the Communist Meyerhold had been dumped, while the non-Communist Stanislavsky still enjoyed the sunlight of official favor.[87] The author (Béla Balász) offered the same sort of explanation for Meyerhold's problems that Bernhard Reich (and many others) had given: Meyerhold's work was no longer relevant; his style was antiquated. All the ideas for which the man was famous—his science of movement, his use of mime and gesture, his heightening of the real into the grotesque, his artistic settings, his emphasis on collective rather than personal psychology—all these had indeed made their contribution to Soviet theater and film. Though others had learned much from him, according to Balász, the teacher himself had nothing more to teach, no further usefulness to Soviet art or to the new society. But Stanislavsky, the great exponent of psychological realism, would always be honored because he had preserved and transferred into Communist society the best elements of bourgeois art. The new Soviet playgoers, so deeply and joyfully immersed in life, want to see life reproduced "directly"; they have no interest in "abstract decorations and rhythms."

"Under such circumstances, should a great theater in a capital city be abandoned to a style which has become the entertainment of an experiment-happy cult of specialists?" Of course, Balász' question was rhetorical. Perhaps Brecht agreed with the implicit answer. Or perhaps the future leader of the Berliner Ensemble, like his hero Herr Keuner, decided to keep his answer in reserve.

NOTES

1. Mordecai Gorelik, "Brecht: 'I am the Einstein of the New Stage Form...,' " *Theatre Arts* 41 (March 1957): 73; Ulrich Weisstein, "From the Dramatic Novel to Epic Theater, a Study of the Contemporary Background of Brecht's Theory and Practice," *The Germanic Review* 38 (May 1963): 270–71 (on the "myth" that Brecht "invented" epic theater and [257–71] Brecht's role in "fusing the many overt and latent trends in the German and European theater of the twenties into a whole"); Stella Arbenina, *Through Terror to Freedom* (London: Hutchinson, 1929?), p. 70.

2. Carl Zuckmayer, *A Part of Myself: Portrait of an Epoch*, trans. Richard and Clara Winston (New York: Harcourt, 1970), p. 233.

3. Joseph Frank, "The Master Linguist" (review of *Dialogues* by Roman Jakobson), *The New York Review of Books* 31 (April 12, 1984): 29. On Russian influence in the development of modern art in the West and particularly in Germany, see: Camilla Gray, *The Russian Experiment in Art: 1863–1922*, 2d ed. (New York: Harry N. Abrams, 1970), pp. 94, 118–19; Robert C. Williams, *Culture in Exile: Russian Emigres in Germany, 1881–1941* (Ithaca, N.Y.: Cornell University Press, 1972), pp. 14–20. For a good survey of the mutual interchange of ideas see Williams' *Artists in Revolution: Portraits of the Russian Avant-Garde, 1905–1925* (Bloomington: Indiana University Press, 1977); Andrei B. Nakov, *Russian Pioneers: At the Origins of Non-Objective Art* (London: Annely Juda Fine Art, 1976), pp. 4–6.

4. Ilya Ehrenburg, *Memoirs: 1921–1941*, trans. Tatania Shebunina and Y. Kapp (New York: Grosset & Dunlap, 1966), p. 18; Williams, *Culture in Exile*, pp. 131–33.

5. Julius Bab, *Das Theater der Gegenwart: Geschichte der dramatischen Bühne seit 1870* (Leipzig: J.J. Weber, 1928), p. 217; Sinclair Dombrow, "The Russian Renaissance in Berlin," *Shadowland* (June 1923): 22–24, 73.

For another article along the same line, see Marie Seton, "Soviet Theatre Down Stream," *Theatre Arts Monthly* 15 (December 1931): 1035–37. This issue also has two photos of Meyerhold productions in Moscow: *The Bedbug* and *The Bathhouse*.

6. IU. P. Murav'ev, "Sovetsko-germanskie sviazi v oblasti literary i isskustva v gody Veimarskoi respubliki," in *Slaviano-germanskie kul'turnye sviazi i otnosheniia*, ed. V. D. Koroliuk (Moscow: Nauka, 1969), pp. 180–81; Erhard Pachaly et al., "Die kulturellen Beziehungen zwischen Deutschland und der Sowjetunion," in *Die grosse sozialistiche Oktober-revolution und Deutschland*, vol. 1, ed. Alfred Anderle et al. (Berlin: Dietz, 1967), p. 450. The German-Russian friendship clubs, their journals and other activities, were communist front organizations directed from Moscow, though many of the "fellow traveler" artists and intellectuals who belonged to, visited, or supported them may not have been aware of that fact. See David Pike, *German Writers in Soviet Exile 1933–1945* (Chapel Hill: The University of North Carolina Press, 1982), pp. 22–24.

7. Joachim Fiebach, "Beziehungen zwischen dem sowjetischen und dem proletarisch-revolutionären Theater der Weimarer Republik," in *Deutschland Sowjetunion*, ed. Heinz Sanke (Berlin: Humboldt-Universität, 1966), p. 425.

8. Some of the more famous members of the society were Heinrich and Thomas Mann, Albert Einstein, Brecht's publisher Ernst Rowohlt, and Käthe Kollwitz. Detailed descriptions of Meyerhold's work appeared in *Das neue Russland* from 1924 through 1926.

9. Fiebach, "Beziehungen," 425; Fritz Mierau, "Die Rezeption der sowjetischen Literatur in Deutschland in den Jahren 1920–24," *Zeitschrift für Slawistik* 3 (1958): 622; Arthur Holitscher, "Drei Monate in Sowjet-Russland," *Die neue Rundschau* 32 (January 1921): 1–32, 121–63, 236–62. The portion of this article dealing with Soviet theater was reprinted in *Das literarische Echo* 23 (March 15, 1921): 743. An enlarged version of Holitscher's article was published in book form by S. Fischer Verlag in 1921 or 1922, soon after its publication in *Die neue Rundschau*. *AIZ* was also a communist front newspaper, one of the many such enterprises of *Mezhrapom* (International Workers' Relief Organization); see Pike, *German Writers*, pp. 22–23.

10. Oscar Blum, "Russische Theaterköpfe. II: Meyerhold," *Die Welt-bühne* (June 22, 1926): 265. Meyerhold used similar Oriental devices in his production of Blok's *The Unknown Woman*. The plays were performed as a double bill in 1914.

11. Bernhard Reich, "Meyerholds neue Inszenierung," *Die literarische Welt* 4, 18 (1928): 7. *Die literarische Welt* was, according to U. Weisstein, "Germany's most intelligently edited and most widely read literary journal of the period" ("From the Dramatic Novel," 270).

12. Guilbeaux, *Les humbles*, 22–23; Nataliia Lunacharskaia-Rozenel', *Pamiat' serdtsa: Vospominaniia* (Moscow: Iskusstvo, 1962), p. 156.

13. Murav'ev, "Sovetsko-germanskie sviazi," 188–89. Edward Braun observes that Meyerhold's early experiments in staging Symbolist drama helped him to arrive "at a new conception of the art of the theatre [which provided] a permanent foundation for his own work, and established a tradition of undisguised artifice and conscious theatricality which Yevreinov, Tairov, Vakhtangov and other directors were later to follow" (*The Theatre of Meyerhold: Revolution on the Modern Stage* [New York: Drama Book Specialists, 1979], p. 86.

14. Eva Kreilisheim, "Brecht und die Sowjetunion," (Ph.D. diss., University of Vienna, 1970), pp. 12–13. For a brief history of Blue Blouse theater, as well as a description of its style, see Christian Mailand-Hansen, *Mejerchol'ds Theaterästhetik in den 1920er Jahren* (Copenhagen: Rosenkilde und Bagger, 1980), pp. 134–36.

15. Harry Wilder, "Die 'Blauen Blusen' und wir," *Das Arbeitertheater* (1928), ms. underlining and marginalia, in Harvard University Houghton Library, Bertolt Brecht Archive 1440/14, Reel 86. Brecht's library also included a copy of Frida Rubiner's essay "Moskauer Theater" which describes the professional theaters (as opposed to workers' troupes). In her article Rubiner described the Moscow Art Theater and the revolutionary productions of the Moscow Trade Union Theater, in Harvard University Houghton Library, Bertolt Brecht Archive 1440/16, Reel 86.

16. Bertolt Brecht, *Schriften zum Theater* (hereafter SzT) 1 (Frankfurt a.M.: Suhrkamp, 1967): 204–05. Meyerhold staged *Roar, China!* in collaboration with his student Vasilii Fedorov.

17. For a detailed account of the historical background of the play, as well as its stage history, see Walter and Ruth Meserve, "The Stage History of *Roar, China!*: Documentary Drama as Propaganda," *Theatre Survey* 21 (May 1980): 1–13; an interesting addition to that article is Alvin Goldfarb's "*Roar China* in a Nazi Concentration Camp," *Theatre Survey* 21 (November 1980): 184–85. An editorial note to Louis Lozowick's "V. E. Meyerhold and His Theater" in *The Hound and Horn* 4 (October-December 1930): 105, announces that "Meyerhold and a company of his actors will present a repertory of five or six plays in New York, starting in January.... The productions will... include *Revisor* and probably *Cocu Magnifique*." The American tour was never realized.

18. N. Velekhova, *Ohklopkov i teatr ulitsa* (Moscow: Isskustvo, 1970), p. 9; Hoover, *Meyerhold*, 264–65, 276; John Fuegi, *The Essential Brecht* (Los Angeles: Hennessy and Ingalls, 1972), pp. 122–23. For a very detailed description of Ohklopkov's production of *Aristocrats*, which combined highly stylized Oriental devices with realistic costumes and

dialogue, see pp. 126–27. John Willett, *Brecht in Context: Comparative Approaches* (London and New York: Methuen, 1984), p. 93.

19. Murav'ev, "Sovetsko-Germanskie sviazi," 190: Gérard Abensour, "Art et politique. La tournée du Théâtre Meyerhold à Paris en 1930," *Cahiers du monde Russe et Soviétique* 17 (April-September 1976): 217–20 has information on the reception of the Meyerhold troupe in Germany and the ensemble's activities there.

20. Hugo Huppert, "Das Taubenhaus," *Neue Deutsche Literatur* 20 (December 1972): 6–34.

21. Bella Chistowa, "Wladimir Majakowskis Beziehungen zu deutschen Literaturschaffenden," *Kunst und Literatur* 9 (1961): 385. Chistowa's source for this information is Horst Knietzch's "Slatan Dudow, Lebensdaten eines sozialistischen Künstlers," *Neues Deutschland* (May 1958). Dudow eventually concentrated on filmmaking. After the war he settled in East Germany, where he "is considered . . . to be one of the most important film producers in the history of realistic cinema" (Yves Aubry, "Slatan Dudow, 1903–1961," *Anthologie du cinéma* 6 [Paris, 1971]: 387–440.

22. My information on the life and work of Anna Lacis is drawn mainly from her memoir, *Revolutionär im Beruf: Berichte über proletarisches Theater, über Meyerhold, Brecht, Benjamin und Piscator*, ed. Hildegard Brenner (Munich: Rogner und Bernhard, 1971). Lacis' teacher V. M. Bekhterev is an important figure in the cultural and intellectual history of early twentieth-century Russia. He ranks with Pavlov as a pioneer researcher on the physiology of mind. Like the later behaviorists, Bekhterev studied mental processes by rigorously and objectively recording their outward manifestations; his deterministic view of behavior emphasized the social and physiological causes of human actions. He founded Russia's first laboratory of experimental psychology in 1895 and the Psychoneurological Institute, Lacis' school, in 1907. The Institute, which quickly became both famous and powerful as an extraordinary educational organization, was "one of the most brilliant achievements of [Bekhterev's] life. . . . The [czarist] authorities . . . regarded the Institute as a hotbed of revolution." (Lacis recalled that Mayakovsky was among the guest lecturers.) Active on many educational, scientific, and social fronts, Bekhterev even gave "such expert evidence in the Beilis case as shattered the hopes of the [government] intriguers." See the introductory essays in Vladimir M. Bekhterev, *General Principles of Human Reflexology* (1932; reprint ed., New York: Arno Press, 1973), pp. i-ii, 5–13, 15–16. Bekhterev's science of reflexology, or objective psychology, had a strong impact on Meyerhold's creative and pedagogical work, including the famous biomechanical exercises for

actors. For a detailed discussion of the influence of Bekhterev and Pavlov on the theories of Meyerhold and Eisenstein, including especially Eisenstein's 1932 essay, "The Montage of Attractions," see Mailand-Hansen, *Mejerchol'ds Theaterästhetik*, pp. 197–208.

23. Lacis, *Revolutionär* pp. 12–13.

24. "The publication took its name from Carlo Gozzi's 'fiaba teatrale,' *The Love of Three Oranges*, of which a free adaptation by Meyerhold, Solovyov and Vogak appeared in the first number. . . . It was Meyerhold who in 1918 gave Prokofiev the idea for the opera of the same name which is based on this translation" (Edward Braun, ed. and trans., *Meyerhold on Theater* [New York: Hill and Wang, 1969], p. 116).

25. Boris Alpers, *Teatr sotsial'noi maski* (Moscow: Gos. izd. khud. lit., 1931), pp. 116–17. English title: *The Theatre of the Social Mask*, trans. Mark Schmidt (New York: Group Theatre, 1934).

26. Lacis *Revolutionär*, p. 21.

27. She had particular success with a children's play written by Meyerhold (based on a story by Oscar Wilde), *Alinur* (*Revolutionär*, p. 24). Bekhterev, *General Principles*, p. 13.

28. Walter Benjamin, "Programm eines proletarischen Kindertheaters," in Lacis, *Revolutionär*, pp. 26–31.

29. Reiner Steinweg, *Das Lehrstück: Brechts Theorie einer politisch-ästhetischen Erziehung* (Stuttgart: J. B. Metzler, 1972), pp. 148–49.

30. Lacis, *Revolutionär*, p. 22.

31. Ibid., p. 37.

32. Bernhard Reich, *Im Wettlauf mit der Zeit: Erinnerungen aus fünf Jarhzehnten deutscher Theatergeschichte* (Berlin: Henschelverlag, 1970), p. 239.

33. According to some observers, the premiere of *The Life of Edward II* was a calamity and there were those who put much of the blame on Anna Lacis. In her memoir she admitted that she literally fell on her face in one scene, where no such action had been called for in the script (*Revolutionär*, p. 39). Rudolf Frank, along with Reich an *Oberspielleiter* of the *Kammerspiele*, recalled bitterly that he tried in vain to persuade her to resign from the cast because of her lack of talent. Moreover, he felt that her Lettish accent, which Brecht prized for its strangeness, created a comic effect where none was intended. Since Lacis refused to resign, Frank resorted to calling her rude names. When that failed he appealed to Brecht and Otto Falckenberg to support him in his plan to fire her, but they refused (Frank, *Spielzeit meines Lebens* [Heidelberg: Lambert Schneider, 1960], pp. 271–73). Frank's opinion that Lacis was untalented was supported by Herbert Ihering's review of the play, in which he referred to her as "the catastrophic actress" (Ihering, *Von*

Reinhardt bis Brecht, Vol. 2, *1924–1929* [Berlin: Aufbau-Verlag, 1959], p. 22). Weisstein in "The First Version of Brecht-Feuchtwanger's *Leben Eduards des Zweiten von England* and Its Relation to the Standard Text" (*Journal of English and Germanic Philology* 69 [April 1970]: 199–200) accepts this unflattering view of Lacis and presumes it was her lack of talent that caused her to be dropped from the cast after opening night. But Otto Falckenberg, who headed the *Kammerspiele* and who had directed Brecht's *Drums in the Night* (1922), had a much more positive impression of Lacis. "Concerning these rehearsals [of *The Life of Edward II*, Falckenberg remembered] above all a 'Russian assistant director, whom Brecht had chosen, a young, incredibly intelligent, unbelievably vital young woman. She worked like crazy deep into the night. When Brecht gave up, the girl came along and began anew. She worked like a young man'" (Wolfgang Petzet, *Theater: Die Münchener Kammerspiele, 1911– 1972* [Munich: Verlag Kurt Desch, 1973], p. 153). By her own account, Lacis suddenly left the cast because, for political reasons, she was forced by the authorities to leave Munich shortly after the play opened. According to her, the "Management" of the *Kammerspiele* had been dead set against having a Communist associated with the theater and had ordered Brecht to fire her, but Brecht refused. There is in Lacis' book the implication that the management's wish to be rid of her and her expulsion from Munich were not unrelated events (*Revolutionär*, p. 38– 39).

34. Lacis, *Revolutionär*, p. 37.

35. Vsevolod Meyerhold, *Liubov k tryom apelsinam* (1914): 4–5, quoted in Braun, *Meyerhold on Theatre*, p. 147.

36. Lacis, *Revolutionär*, pp. 41–42, 49, 54; Benjamin, *Briefe*, vol. 1, ed. Gershom Scholem and Theodor W. Adorno (Frankfurt a.M.: Suhrkamp, 1966), p. 440; Benjamin, *Moskauer Tagebuch*, ed. Gershom Scholem (Frankfurt a.M.: Suhrkamp, 1980), pp. 13, 85.

37. Benjamin, "Der Regisseur Meyerhold—in Moskau erledigt?," *Die literarische Welt* (February 11, 1927): 3. It is interesting to compare Benjamin's and Lacis' eyewitness accounts of this public discussion because their memories of it are so disparate. According to Benjamin, the debate was held in Meyerhold's theater (which was very small) and failed miserably in its goal of rallying public opinion to the director. In Lacis' memoir the event took place in "a great hall," was attended by "thousands," and was a huge victory for the pro-Meyerhold forces (*Revolutionär*, pp. 54–55).

38. Lacis, *Revolutionär*, p. 58.

39. *Pervyi vsesoiuznyi s'ezd sovetskikh pisatelei* (1934), p. 345. "Bertolt Brecht und die sowjetische Kunst und Literatur," *Geschichte der rus-*

sischen Sowjetliteratur 1917–1941, ed. Harri Jünger et al. (Berlin: Akademie-Verlag, 1973), pp. 610–11. The author of this article (probably
Gudrun Düwel) claims that Tretiakov's introduction to his *B. Brekht:
epischeskie dramy* (Moscow, 1934), pp. 3–22), gives evidence of an acquaintance dating back to the twenties. Anna Lacis recalled that in
Berlin in 1928 Brecht asked her about Tretiakov and once again ques-
tioned her closely about the directing methods of Meyerhold and Tairov, as well as about Marxist criticism and art theory "and naturally
about life in the Soviet Union" (*Revolutionär*, p. 58). According to an
article written by Tretiakov, the visit of Brecht and Dudow was sponsored by the (Soviet) Journal-Newspaper Society and the two planned
to stay one week ("Bert Brekht," *Literaturnaia gazeta* [May 12, 1932]).

40. *Bertolt Brecht: Poems, 1913–1956*, 2d ed., ed. John Willett and Ralph
Manheim (London: Methuen, 1979), pp. 331–33.

41. Aleksandr V. Fevral'skii, "S. M. Tret'iakov v teatre Meierkhol'-
da," in Sergei Tret'iakov, *Slyshish' Moskva?!*, ed. G. Mokrusheva (Moscow: Iskusstvo, 1966), pp. 187–88. Mailand-Hansen, *Mejerchol'ds
Theaterästhetik*, p. 99.

42. Tret'iakov, *B. Brekht: epischeskie dramy* (Moscow-Leningrad, 1934);
International Literature 3 (Moscow, July 1933): 139–40.

43. Tretjakow, *Ich will ein Kind haben (Die Pionierin)*, trans. Ernst Hube,
adapted by Bert Brecht (Freiberg im Breisgau: Max Reichard-Verlag,
n.d.), "als Manuskript vervielfältigt" (c. 1930). Brecht never did produce
Tretiakov's play. The Reichard-Verlag acting script is a translation of
the second version of the play, and has a more open-ended, less upbeat
ending than the first version. Meyerhold and Tretiakov were never able
to get either draft past the Soviet censors, though they tried for four
years (1926–1930). At about the same time, the prominent Soviet director Igor Terentev was also interested in staging *I Want a Baby* (Russian
title: *Khochu rebenka*), also to no avail. As far as I know, the only production of the play occurred in 1980 at the Badisches Stadtstheater in
Karlsruhe, in a translation by Fritz Mierau, who kindly sent me the
playbill, according to which Gerhardt-Verlag (Berlin) has published a
volume which includes both versions of *I Want a Baby*.

44. *International Literature* 3 (July 1933): 140. The Bertolt Brecht Archive has a letter in which Tretiakov raised various objections to the
content of Brecht's *St. Joan of the Stockyards*, and also has a letter from
Piscator to Brecht, written from the USSR, in which Piscator says that
Tretiakov has made many changes in *St. Joan*; see Marjorie Hoover,
"Brecht's Soviet Connection: Tretiakov," *Brecht Heute/Brecht Today* 3,
ed. Gisela Bahr et al. (Frankfurt a.M.: Athenäum, 1973): 49.

45. Benjamin, *Understanding Brecht*, pp. 10–11.

46. For a history and discussion of Shklovsky's use of the terms *ostranenie* and *otchuzhdenie*, see Renate Lachmann, "Die 'Verfremdung' und das 'neue Sehen' bei Viktor Šklovskij," *Poetica* 3 (January- April 1970): 226–49. To support his thesis that avant-garde theater was reborn in the Soviet Union in the mid-1950s and 1960s by way of Brecht, Efim Etkind gives a nutshell history of the "comical" *ostranenie-Verfremdung-otchuzhdenie* transformations ("Brecht and the Soviet Theater," pp. 81–87).

47. Reich, *Wettlauf*, pp. 371–72. Shklovsky agreed that his concept of *ostranenie* came to Brecht by way of Tretiakov. See Ilja Fradkin, *Bertolt Brecht, Weg und Methode* (Leipzig: Philipp Reclam jun., 1977), p. 153. Fradkin's source for this information is Vladimir Pozner's interview of Shklovsky in *Les lettres françaises*, 31 December 1964 to 6 January 1965, p. 6.

48. John Willett, *The Theatre of Bertolt Brecht. A Study from Eight Aspects*, 3d ed., rev. (New York: New Directions, 1968), p. 178. Willett's theory is based on the fact that "conception and catchword alike only enter [Brecht's] work after his first [second] visit to Moscow in 1935."

49. The idea that there is a direct relationship between Shklovsky's *ostranenie* and Brecht's *Verfremdung* may now be gaining acceptance among East German scholars. In their biography of Brecht the Schumachers seem to accept Willett's thesis and Reich's recollection, noting only that Shklovsky was not primarily concerned with the possibility of using *ostranenie* as a tool for social reform (Ernst Schumacher and Renate Schumacher, *Leben Brechts in Wort und Bild* [Berlin: Henschelverlag Kunst und Gesellschaft, 1978], p. 129). The linguistic argument is that Shklovsky's *priem ostraneniia* does not really translate into *Verfremdungseffekt* but into *Seltsammachen*, and so on. On the other hand, Brecht probably was not particularly concerned about precise translation.

50. Jan Knopf, *Bertolt Brecht; ein kritischer Forschungsbericht: Fragwürdiges in der Brecht-Forschung* (Frankfurt a.M.: Athenäum, 1974), pp. 15–20; E. J. Brown, "The Formalist Contribution," *The Russian Review* 33 (July 1974): 244, 253.

51. "Bert Brekht v Moskve," *Pravda* (April 23, 1935): 4; or see the Brecht interview in *Deutsche Zentral-Zeitung*, Moscow (May 23, 1935). The latter article is cited in Schumacher's *Leben Brechts*, p. 129.

52. *SzT* 4: 56–57; *SzT* 5 (c. 1937): 169.

53. *SzT* 4: 58.

54. Meierkhol'd, *Stat'i, pis'ma, rechi, besedy* (hereafter *SPRB*), vol. 2, *1917–1939* (Moscow: Iskusstvo, 1968), p. 322.

55. A. C. Scott, *Mei Lan-fang: Leader of the Pear Garden* (Hong Kong: Hong Kong University Press, 1959), pp. 117–18.

56. "O gastroliakh Mei Lan'-fana," *Tvorcheskoe nasledie V. E. Meier-khol'da*, ed. L. D. Vendrovskaia and A. V. Fevral'skii (Moscow: Vseross. teatral. obsh., 1978), pp. 95–97.

57. "Vsevolod Meierkhol'd," *LEF* (April-May 1923): 169.

58. *Feld-Herren: Der Kampf um eine Kollectivwirtschaft*, trans. Rudolf Selke (Berlin: Malik-Verlag, 1931). *Feld-Herren* is a combination and condensation of two books by Tretiakov: *Vyzov: Kolkhoznye ocherki* (*The Challenge: Collective Farm Sketches*) (Moscow: Federatsiia, 1930), and *Mesiats v derevne (jun-jul 1930 g.): Operativnye ocherki* (*A Month in the Country, June-July 1930: Operative Essays*) (Moscow: Federatsiia, 1930). See Fritz Mierau, *Erfindung und Korrektur: Tretjakows Ästhetik der Operativität* (Berlin: Akademie-Verlag, 1976), p. 108. This book contains as appendix the text of *Ich will ein Kind haben* (pp. 179–246), and letters from Tretiakov to Brecht during the years 1933–1937 (pp. 258–72).

59. Brecht, *SzT* 1 (1931): 243–61; *SzT* 7 (1950s): 221–331. Fritz Mierau, "Sergei Tret'jakov und Bertolt Brecht. Das Produktionsstück *Khochu rebenka* (zweite Fassung)," *Zeitschrift für Slawistik* 20 (1975): 229, 235, 240–41.

60. Cited by Fevral'skii, in S. Tret'iakov, *Slyshish', Moskva?!*, pp. 203–04. In 1928, Terentev published his plan for staging Tretiakov's debate drama. The plan included a glass booth with microphone onstage. From inside the booth a master of ceremonies would field questions from the audience. See Mierau, *Zeitschrift für Slawistik*: 237.

61. Benjamin, "Der Autor als Produzent," *Versuche über Brecht* (Frankfurt a.M.: Suhrkamp, 1966), p. 99. A translation of Tretiakov's first version of *Khochu rebenka* is in *Sergei Tretjakow: Ich will ein Kind haben; Brülle, China!*, trans. and ed. Fritz Mierau (Berlin: Henschelverlag, 1976).

62. Renata Berg-Pan, "Mixing Old and New Wisdom: The 'Chinese' Sources of Brecht's *Kaukasischer Kreidekreis* and Other Works," *The German Quarterly* 48 (March 1975): 221; Claude Hill, *Bertolt Brecht* (Boston: Twayne, 1975), pp. 137–38; Eric Bentley, *Seven Plays by Bertolt Brecht* (New York: Grove, 1961), p. xlviii.

63. Kopelev, *Brekht*, p. 209.

64. Howard R. Holter, "The Legacy of Lunacharsky and Artistic Freedom in the USSR," *Slavic Review* 29 (June 1970): 265–66; see also A. L. Tait, "Lunacharsky, the 'Poet-Commissar,'" *The Slavonic and East European Review* 52 (April 1974): 234–51; Claude Frioux, "Lunačarskij et le futurisme Russe," *Cahiers du monde Russe et Soviétique* 1 (January-March 1960): 307–18. This last essay especially gives an interesting and balanced view of Lunacharsky's relation to the Futurists. Frioux does not gloss over the commissar's hostility to many Futurists and aspects of Futurism, yet stresses his capacity to admire the work of individual

Futurists, especially that of Mayakovsky and Meyerhold, and to separate his personal opinions from his political power as censor.

65. Braun, *Meyerhold on Theatre*, p. 160.

66. Lunacharsky, "Esche o teatre Meierkhol'da" (1926), *Sobranie sochinenii* (hereafter *Sob. soch.*) 3 (Moscow: "Khudozhestvennaia Lit.,"
1964): 303.

67. Lunacharskii, "Zabludivshiisia iskatel' " (1908), *Sob. soch.* 3: 28.

68. "Meyerhold . . . can profit better than anyone else [by the use of
grotesquerie], which affords the possibility of showing reality as even
more real than it appears in life," in "Teatr Meierkhol'da" (1926), *Sob.
soch.* 3: 301.

69. Lunacharskii, "*Revizor* Gogolia-Meierkohl'da," *Sob. soch.* 3: 362.

70. Lunacharskaia-Rozenel', *Pamiat' serdtsa*, pp. 154–57.

71. Lunacharskii, "Na tri grosha" (1928), *O teatre i dramaturgii* 2 (Moscow: Iskusstvo, 1958): 368–70; Dora Angres, *Die Beziehungen Lunachar-
skijs zur deutschen Literatur* (Berlin: Akademie-Verlag, 1970), p. 194.

72. Lunacharskii, "Na tri grosha," pp. 368–69.

73. Alpers, *Teatr sotsial'noi maski*, p. 97.

74. Anna Lacis, *Revoliutsionnyi teatr Germanii*, trans. from German
ms. by N. Barkhash (Moscow, 1935), p. 250. Many of the German
workers' theater troupes travelled to Moscow and Leningrad to learn
the playwriting and acting style of TRAM; see Fiebach, "Beziehungen,"
p. 430.

75. Lunacharskaia-Rozenel', *Pamiat' serdtsa*, p. 162.

76. According to Marianne Kesting, "When Brecht stayed in Moscow
in 1936, he is said to have gone to Meyerhold's Studio and attended
rehearsals there, day after day" (*Entdeckung und Destruktion: Zur Strukturumwandlung der Künste* [Munich: Wilhelm Fink, 1970], p. 244). Here,
Kesting does not give the source of her information, and I have seen
no other reference to any sort of direct contact between Brecht and
Meyerhold during 1936 or any other time. In her article "Wagner/Mey-
erhold/Brecht," *Brecht Jahrbuch 1977*, ed. J. Fuegi et al., (Frankfurt a.M.:
Suhrkamp, 1977), p. 129, she gives the same information, attributing
it to an "oral communication given to me by the Russian translator
Alexander Kaempfe, Munich." However, no mention is made of the
year—the information is given in a footnote on Brecht's activities in
Moscow in 1935. *Das Wort* (July 1936–March 1939), a journal of the
German literary popular front, was published in Moscow, under the
nominal editorship of Feuchtwanger, Brecht, and Willi Bredel. Bredel,
the only one of the three resident in Moscow, should have been the
most active editor, but he left to attend a writers' congress in Spain,
then went to Paris. So the bulk of the editorial work from 1937 until

the journal's liquidation was taken over by Fritz Erpenbeck (a former actor who had appeared in *Kuhle Wampe*). After the war, Erpenbeck returned to East Germany where he became a powerful drama critic, hostile to Brecht's work. Brecht's 1936 Moscow trip on behalf of *Das Wort* apparently occurred only in Lunacharskaia's imagination. At least, I have not found any corroborating evidence that Brecht went to Moscow that year (or at any other time) because of *Das Wort*. Pike's *German Writers in Soviet Exile* devotes an entire chapter to *Das Wort* and those involved with its publication. In a footnote Pike observes that "In July [1936] Brecht had evidently thought of going to Moscow and assuming editorial responsibilities, at least for several months" (pp. 211–12).

77. Lunacharskaia-Rozenel', *Pamiat' serdtsa*, p. 164. Dora Angres thinks that in certain respects Lunacharskaia's rosy picture of the relationship between Brecht and the commissar is not to be trusted. In particular Angres disputes those passages which "give the impression that Lunacharskii recognized Brecht's significance, and predicted a great future for him" (Angres, *Die Beziehungen*, p. 195). Angres believes such an impression is not compatible with the fact that Lunacharskii, a wondrously prolific writer, had almost nothing to say about Brecht in print. Lunacharskii first wrote about Brecht in his 1928 review of *The Threepenny Opera* and only once again, just in passing, in 1932, in an article on "The Twilight of the Bourgeois Theater" (*Sob. soch.* 6: 494). "Either he knew no other works of [Brecht] or—and this is much more likely—Brecht's skeptical non-illusion concerning the expressionistic rhetoric of redemption, as it is somewhat exaggeratedly manifested in the figure of Kragler, contradicted [Lunacharskii's] esthetic views so strongly, that he did not understand Brecht's intentions and probably even viewed them as an attack on avantgardism in literature. He disregarded the philosophical discussions in Brecht's work. In a conversation with [Dora Angres], A. I. Dejč revealed that Lunacharskii thought Brecht's writing was affected [*gekünstelt*]. . . . In any case . . . the picture which Lunacharskaia-Rozenel' presents must, in essential points, be rejected as incorrect" (Angres, *Die Beziehungen*, p. 196).

78. See Ellendea Proffer's "Introduction" to Konstantin Rudnitsky, *Meyerhold the Director*, trans. George Petrov, ed. Sydney Schultze (Ann Arbor, Mich.: Ardis, 1981), p. xv.

79. Klaus Völker, *Brecht-Chronik: Daten zu Leben und Werk* (Munich: Carl Hanser, 1971), p. 86; Reich, *Wettlauf*, p. 376. According to the Schumachers' research, however, Brecht met with many German friends while in Moscow at that time (*Leben Brechts*, p. 159).

80. Kopelev, *Brekht*, 236.

81. John Willett, *Brecht in Context* (London and New York: Methuen,

1984), p. 238. Rudnitsky (*Meyerhold the Director*, p. 209) discusses the influence Meyerhold had on *Princess Turandot* and other famous Vakhtangov productions. According to Fuegi (*The Essential Brecht*, p. 257) Brecht was wont to encode his politically sensitive writings on theater and "Vakhtangov" was a safe word for avant-garde theater.

82. Bertolt Brecht, undated fragmentary letter written at Svendborg (Harvard University Houghton Library, Bertolt Brecht Archive, Folder 1396).

83. Brecht, *The Messingkauf Dialogues*, ed. and trans. John Willett (London: Methuen, 1965), pp. 68–69; *SzT* 3 (1930s): 17–18, 119.

84. Hoover, *Meyerhold*, p. 260.

85. *SzT* 3 (1939): 85–86.

86. *SzT* 3 (c. 1935): 16, 51–52, 103, 214; 2 (1935–36): 175; 1 (1926): 188. See also Brecht's "Kölner Rundfunkgespräch," in which he claimed to have originated the theory of epic theater but allowed that there were precedents to his work: the beginnings of nineteenth-century European naturalism, and the theaters of China and India (*SzT* 1: 123). In 1924 Piscator staged Paquet's *Fahnen* (*Flags*) as "epic theater" (Kesting, "Wagner," pp. 128–29).

87. *SzT* 3 (1939): 80, 103; Béla Balász, "Meyerhold und Stanislawsky," *Das Wort* 7, 5 (May 1938): 115–21.

2

"EVERYONE SEES ME AND I SEE EVERYONE"

Brecht met one of his earliest and most important informants on Soviet theater in 1923, just when he was preparing (for the second time) to direct a play.[1] The play was *The Life of Edward II of England*, adapted from Marlowe's *Edward II* by Brecht and Lion Feuchtwanger for presentation at the Munich *Kammerspiele*. The informant was Anna Lacis, who assisted in the production and played Edward's son. Both she and Bernhard Reich have written that Brecht was eager to learn as much as possible about the latest developments in Soviet theater. Lacis was well informed about this matter and especially about the work of Meyerhold, whose name in the 1920s was synonymous with avantgarde theater. What sort of information would Brecht have gotten from Lacis?

Meyerhold's first attempt at non-representational staging occurred in 1903 with his production of Przybyszewski's *Snow* and von Schönthan's *The Acrobats*, staged by his own troupe, The Fellowship of the New Drama, a group he organized after his departure from the Moscow Art Theater in 1902.

In general, Meyerhold's experiments from 1903 to about 1908 represent his attempts to find methods of staging Symbolist drama.[2] The productions of his Symbolist period used colors, to establish a mood and symbolize the essence of a character or event, and music, to intensify that mood. It was a slow-motion theater of carefully orchestrated poses and ritualistic gestures, enacted upon a shallow stage against a flat, monotonal background which made the actors look like figures carved in low relief.[3]

Meyerhold began to experiment consistently with new forms from 1905. In that year Stanislavsky (who was himself searching for methods of staging Symbolist drama) decided to organize a small theater especially for experimentation. This was a unique idea at the time, and Meyerhold, whom Stanislavsky had chosen to direct the experiment, invented a new phrase to describe the concept. He called it a theater studio.[4] But because of disagreements between Meyerhold and Stanislavsky, the studio enterprise lasted only a year, and its productions were never shown to the public.

Symbolist drama has an important similarity to realistic theater. Like the realists, the dramatic Symbolists want to persuade playgoers that what they are seeing, though fantastic, is "real." In both cases, actors and directors try to maintain the "fourth wall" barrier between audience and stage. When Meyerhold abandoned Symbolist drama, what he rejected was theater as illusion and quasi-religious ritual (dark auditorium, weak stage lighting, distinct separation between audience and stage). Still, the break away from slavish reproduction of everyday reality was taught him by Symbolist drama and remained a guiding principle of his career ever after. The Symbolist portrayal of dreamlife and fairy tale was transmuted into the unabashed theatricality of "conscious" theater.[5]

One of the studio productions was Maeterlinck's *Death of Tintagiles*. Sapunov and Sudeikin, the artists working on it, could not construct scale models of the setting (Stanislavsky's hallowed method). Being artists rather than professional stage carpenters, they simply did not know how to glue models together. So Meyerhold suggested they skip the models and draw sketches. This method turned out to be just right for Symbolist theater, which needed, not scale-model reproductions of reality, but "impressionist plans" which would only *suggest* the atmosphere of a time or place.[6] From that time forward, Meyerhold relied mainly on sketches as preparation for his settings. The principle of suggestion became one of the crucial means by which the new theater could reach out to its audience and bring it within the creative circle.[7]

The effects of this evocative method were evident in the production plans for the studio plays. For example, in Hauptmann's *Colleague Krampton* the atmosphere of an artist's garret was evoked by the use of a single huge canvas which dominated half the stage. The audience could hardly notice anything else, except perhaps the edge of a skylight, a bit of sky, and here and there, some objects inevitably found in an artist's workroom: sketches, a stepladder, a table. Meyerhold claimed that *Colleague Krampton* introduced the principle of stylized theater, a principle which was further advanced by the studio production of Hauptmann's *Schluck and Jau*. Instead of trying to recreate eighteenth-century French rooms, halls, and gardens, the artists used "powerful brush-strokes" to suggest the era. Huge, flower-decked castle gates at the very front of the stage were meant to "startle the audience with their grandioseness, their vastness and their splendor."[8] Beyond these gates, the audience was supposed to imagine an eighteenth-century estate and a whole aristocratic way of life.

Suggesting the atmosphere of a time or place by a construction of elaborate doors or gates would appear again and again in Meyerhold's work. In "the first Soviet comedy," Mayakovsky's *Mystery-Bouffe* (1917), Hell and Heaven were represented mainly by their huge portals, forerunners of the department store revolving doors in Act I of Mayakovsky's *The Bedbug* (1929). Meyerhold's production of Tchaikovsky's *The Queen of Spades* (1935) began with a view of "beautiful wrought-iron gates, typical of old Petersburg."[9]

In another *Schluck and Jau* scene, the royal bedroom was suggested by a ridiculously elaborate bed and canopy. Meyerhold's technique of suggesting opulence through exaggeration was later used effectively in his staging of *The Inspector General* (1926) and *Camille* (1934). For *Schluck and Jau*, he also used the device of multiple uniformity as a means of caricaturing a social class: identical ladies seated in identical bowers sew on a single length of ribbon, keeping exact time to the strains of an eighteenth-century duet.

After his departure from the Art Theater Studio in 1906, Meyerhold briefly rejoined The Fellowship of the New Drama. While directing for that group, he presented shows which featured a single constructed setting, a deep forestage, no front curtain (the latter was a sensational departure from tradition[10]), and dance-like movements inspired by Japanese theater. But the fellowship soon lost its bold director to Vera Komissarzhevskaia. She was a deeply talented and enormously popular actress who had established her own ensemble and was searching for new methods and an innovative director. Meyerhold gladly accepted this chance to carry out his experiments with a major ensemble in a capital city.

The relationship between Meyerhold and Komissarzhevskaia was a troubled one and lasted only one season. But some of the fruits of that association were remarkable, and did indeed mark the beginning of a new stage in the history of Russian theater. Criticism of Meyerhold's work at Komissarzhevskaia's theater was often ferocious, but here and there some critics perceived the significance of his experiments.[11]

There was the landmark production of Alexander Blok's *The Fairground Booth*, a parody of Symbolist drama, in which an entire little theater was constructed onstage with its own "audience," and an Author who commented on the action and generally made a nuisance of himself. All the backstage machinery and paraphernalia were revealed to the audience, including pulleys, catwalks, and so on, usually hidden above the stage. When the scenery was raised in the little theater, the real audience could see how it all worked. In front of the little theater was an open space, occupied by the Author, who was a "kind of liaison between the public and the action on the little stage," and who from time to time "interpolates puerile remarks."[12] At the beginning of the play he runs to the front of the stage and begins a long speech, but "someone unseen pulls him by his coattails back behind the wings; he is shown to be tied by a rope so he cannot interrupt the solemn proceedings onstage."[13] Thus did Meyerhold and Blok help to destroy the Symbolist drama they had been so instrumental in creating. Moreover, *The Fairground Booth* was Meyerhold's first experiment in revealing what Boris Alpers called "the kitchen side" of the play. Now playgoers could get some technical knowledge of theater, thus "implant[ing] a critical attitude toward the stage."[14]

With Andrevev's *The Life of a Man* (1906), Meyerhold introduced area lighting to the Russian theater,[15] a technique he repeated for Wedekind's *Spring's Awakening* (1907) and used, in one variation or another, throughout his career. Commenting on the parallels between Cubist painting and jazz and the avantgarde theater of the twenties, Boris Zingerman, a Soviet critic, observed that "the epic montage theater has . . . neither depths nor perspective. Everything is shoved into the foreground, and just as close as possible to the spectator."[16] Meyerhold's introduction of bright, even lighting for auditorium and stage pioneered this tendency to eliminate depth and perspective, and perhaps also drew the audience and performers closer together psychologically. For Calderón's *Adoration of the Cross* (1910 and 1912) the stage was lit from above and from the sides.[17]

The change from the pale, weak lighting of his Symbolist period in favor of brightly and evenly lit stage and auditorium was a natural result of Meyerhold's continuing drive to break down "fourth wall" illusionism, and return theater to its ancient function as a center of communal festivity. Evidently, auditorium lights were kept on in Blok's *The Unknown Woman* (1914),[18] as also in *The Dawns* (1920). *The Forest* (1924) left nothing in the dark; "hard glittering lights" revealed "every corner of the stage-space in all its crudeness of brick and metal, paint and canvas." These experiments with bold, bright lighting made possible experiments with quick scene changes. Meyerhold is said to be the first director to use light versus dark as a means of quickly presenting a series of brief episodes. For his production of Wedekind's *Spring's Awakening* (1907), the stage was set from the beginning for all eighteen episodes. The action was divided into segments by illuminating small parts of the stage, leaving the rest of the stage completely dark. A spotlight might pick out a bed and chair, a short dialogue followed—the light momentarily went out—then on again to pick out another scene.[19] For *The Earth Rampant* (1923), Meyerhold used military searchlights. And for one of his last major productions, *Camille* (1935), bare spotlights were mounted on platforms in different parts of the auditorium.[20]

The removal of the front curtain, the use of full white lighting, the revelation of the stage "kitchen" were only the beginning of a long list of innovations introduced by Meyerhold to the

Russian stage during the brief time he worked at the Art Theater Studio and with Komissarzhevskaia. In 1907 he was not allowed to present Maeterlinck's *Pelleas and Melisande* in the round, so he compromised by placing the actors on a "raised platform in the middle of a conventional stage, surrounded by the orchestra."[21] For Sologub's *Victory of Death* (1907), anticipating the style of the German Expressionist director Leopold Jessner, Meyerhold built a flight of steps the full width of the stage, and the action took place on these steps. He wanted to extend the steps into the auditorium but was again denied permission.

At this time (1907) Meyerhold wrote that the use of suggestive rather than imitative settings would promote the intellectual participation of the audience in the performance. If everything is set out before the spectators ready-made, the audience's creative abilities are neither motivated nor needed. Therefore (so Meyerhold's argument ran), the settings should be kept to a minimum, each item being crucial and having an important symbolic and practical use in the production. The setting then becomes part of the relationship among the characters in the play. "The spectator must remember some unusual contour of a divan, a grandiose column, some gilded mirrors, a bookcase along the whole wall, a vast buffet, and with these separate parts [the playgoer] fills in the rest with his imagination."[22]

Shortly after he parted from Komissarzhevskaia, Meyerhold was appointed a stage director and actor at the Petersburg Imperial Theaters, posts which he held from 1908 until 1917. For his production of Wagner's *Tristan and Isolde* (1909) Meyerhold showed that the sort of simplified, stylized setting he advocated could be used even when the author had had something quite different in mind. Wagner's trite stage directions were simply ignored. For the third act, the composer had specified a stage crammed with properties (tall palatial structures, parapets with watchtowers, castles, and so on). Meyerhold's artist replaced all that with a "cheerless wide horizon and the mournful, bare cliffs of Brittany."[23] For the second act scene in which Tristan places his beloved Isolde on a bank of flowers, Meyerhold refused to allow any vegetation; to do so would have been "just as glaringly tasteless as illustrating the pages of Edgar Allan Poe." The director supported his decision by pointing to the writings of cer-

tain German theoreticians: the early nineteenth-century dramatist
and theater reformer Karl Immermann[24] and the *Kaffeehausliterat*
Peter Altenberg, one of the leading spokesmen of Viennese
Impressionism. Immermann had emphasized the importance of
exploiting the audience's imaginative abilities; Altenberg con-
curred: "To say a lot with a little—indeed this is the essential
point.... The Japanese draw one flowering twig and that is the
whole spring. We draw the whole spring and it is not even a
flowering twig!"[25]

As he had done with *The Life of a Man* at Komissarzhevskaia's
theater in 1907, Meyerhold staged (in a private house, for a few
friends) Calderón's *Adoration of the Cross* with no settings at all,
in the usual sense, "only those objects which helped the actors
in their acting and which would best express the spirit of Calderón. The stage was constructed to look like a large white tent;
through its back portion, laid open in narrow vertical strips, the
actors entered and exited."[26] In one scene, the actors were supposed to be tied to trees, but Meyerhold's production included
neither trees nor ties. The actors "simply leaned against two
columns at the front of the stage . . . a rope draped across their
arms." Another actor wrapped himself in a curtain to signify a
peasant hiding in a bush.[27]

On the eve of the 1917 February revolution, Meyerhold presented his version of Lermontov's *Masquerade*. He changed the
five-act structure into ten episodes—a fragmenting technique
which became notorious as a hallmark of his productions. In his
essay "The Reconstruction of the Theater," Meyerhold advocated eliminating the traditional division of plays into acts, suggesting instead the division into episodes and scenes, which
characterized Shakespearean and Golden Age Spanish theater,
in order "to surmount the stagnation of the pseudoclassical unity
of action and time."[28] Thus from 1917 to almost the end of his
career in 1934 when he staged *Camille*, the move away from the
longer act as the basic structural unit, toward a series of short,
more or less independent episodes, was a staple device. Meyerhold tended to divide each act into "bits" (*kuski*), in a manner
quite foreign to traditional theater as practiced, for instance, at
the Moscow Art Theater. There, segments of a play were re-
hearsed separately, but in performance blended in order to pro-

duce the effect of smooth continuity. By contrast, Meyerhold staged each small episode so that it was clearly distinguishable from the others. Each "bit" had its own title, was sometimes played as a separate scene with a pause before and after, was sometimes introduced by music, and sometimes had its own setting, "none of this specified by the author, be it understood."[29]

The creator of the Symbolist theater in Russia, Meyerhold was the first director to use the interrelated styles of the Cubo-Futurists and Constructivists in Russian theater. Though Apollinaire's 1913 *Les peintres cubistes* is said to be the main influence on Cubist stage design, Meyerhold's staging of Przybyszewski's *Eternal Fairy Tale* at Komissarzhevskaia's theater in 1906 must have been one of the first, if not the first, uses of Cubist style in theater: a mythical village constructed of cubes, a ladder, round pillars, and square columns to create windows and a door. His staging of "the first Soviet comedy," Mayakovsky's *Mystery-Bouffe*, had two major presentations, 1917 and 1921. The settings were entirely abstract and showed the influence of various avant-garde movements in the Russian art of the period. For the 1917 production, "the painter Malevich put on the boards a huge blue hemisphere representing the terrestrial globe and some cubic forms intimating the Ark. The hell was a Gothic green-red hall; the paradise, a gray cardboard construction with multi-colored clouds; and the promised land, a structure of machines." For the first staging of this comedy, Meyerhold entirely did away with the proscenium as well as with the front curtain and flown scenery.[30]

Erast Garin, who was one of Meyerhold's principal actors, has described the startling effect of the 1921 production in which "half of a vast 'watermelon' representing Earth, occupied the whole right hand part of the stage and, not having enough space there, it displaced the first row of seats." Two-foot-high letters on the half globe announced "ZEMLIA" (Earth). "The left side of the stage was filled with simple platforms, extending upward, into the depths of the theater boxes."[31] The huge hemisphere revolved so that the exit from Hell was revealed. At the end of the play, the audience was invited to come onstage to join the actors. What most impressed Garin upon first seeing *Mystery-Bouffe* was the sense of spatial freedom and openness. There were no cloth hangings or heavy scenery to obscure the view of the stage.

In short, the *Mystery-Bouffe* settings were done in that Cubist-Suprematist style which had such a strong impact on stage design in the West, not the least in Germany, in the 1920s.[32] The philosophy of the Constructivist artists who worked with Meyerhold demanded that the settings have a utilitarian as well as a decorative value, and in his productions the various wheels and ramps, staircases and panels, actually did become an important part of the action and, at times, like the music and gestures, helped to express unspoken emotions. For example, in *The Magnanimous Cuckold* (1922) giant windmills turned ever faster as the psychological tension mounted, or a lover slid down a great curved slide in order to show his joy at meeting his sweetheart. The famous moving walls in *Trust D. E.* (1924)—panels mounted on wheels—closed in on a character when he felt frightened and trapped. Devices such as these bodied forth ideas and emotional states.

In Meyerhold's artistic history the geometric settings had a lasting influence, though later they were replaced by or interspersed with plain, simple background settings, often of panels (movable or fixed) which enclosed a stage area furnished with a few carefully chosen properties. Often, these properties were specially constructed so that their color and form were heightened and exaggerated.

After the October Revolution, Meyerhold put more emphasis on the relevance of theater to social issues than he had done before, a shift of focus which was natural enough, given the radically altered historical circumstance. But Meyerhold's pre-revolutionary writings show that his concern for the relationship between theater and social problems was not born at the moment of the Bolshevik victory. He had, in 1901, travelled with the Art Theater troupe to St. Petersburg, where he witnessed a bloody clash between students and police. The incident left him both shaken and excited. He was outraged at the police action, but also amazed to discover the theater itself involved. The play the Art Theater troupe presented the evening following the demonstration was Ibsen's *An Enemy of the People*. Students who had been battered by police the night before crowded into the theater

and wildly cheered those parts of the dialogue which seemed
appropriate to their struggle. Afterward, Meyerhold wrote to
his adored friend Chekhov: "I want to burn with the spirit of
my time. I want all those who belong to the theater to achieve
a consciousness of their high mission. I am upset by my comrades' not wanting to rise above narrow caste interests foreign
to the interests of society. Yes, theater can play a great role in
the reconstruction of all society!"[33]

Recognition of the power of theater to galvanize an audience
politically is just one aspect of the idea that spectators can in
some sense participate in the production of a work of art. Perhaps one of the things that made Meyerhold's involvement with
Symbolism so short-lived was his realization that the mystical,
almost religious atmosphere of Symbolist drama presupposes a
passive, intellectually anesthetized audience. The thrust of his
work, for almost forty years, was toward the melding of audience
and stage, both physically (the stage extending into the auditorium, claques of actors in the hall, and so on) and intellectually
(the development of a montage theater, in which disparate artistic elements are presented and the playgoer's imagination has
to fill in the gaps). This theatrical philosophy had its problems,
however. Meyerhold wanted to have the audience as creative
partner, but he also wanted to teach and influence the audience.
What happens when the tastes and demands of the playgoers
and the director-artist don't happen to coincide? Then the director, in his greater experience and wisdom, must have the last
word.

In an essay written in 1909, Meyerhold pictured audiences as
being generally bad for theater when they determine what gets
written and staged. The young director claimed that when the
public takes over, the theater usually has to serve one of two
masters: sheer entertainment, or sheer political agitation, "dog-
matism or diversion." To have outstanding theater, the best
artists, not the public, must be in control, to elevate and educate
the tastes of the masses.[34]

But whatever Meyerhold thought about the level of intellect
or expertise of his audience, his productions reflected, from early
on, a ceaseless effort to reach out to them, to include them
intellectually in the artistic effort, and to let them in on all the

theater's tricks. To achieve physical closeness to the audience, a director can thrust the stage forward into the auditorium, bridge over the orchestra, remove the footlights, and shift the action itself forward from back center stage to the very edge of the proscenium. When Meyerhold did this, at the Imperial Theater (in 1907 for *Don Juan*), the old actor Varlamov, who played Sganarelle and who regarded with hostility any new ideas which might disturb him in his old age, was absolutely delighted: " 'Here's a real director!' " (he crowed) " 'He doesn't seat me [Varlamov, because of his age and reluctance to stray far from the prompter, remained seated during most of the play] . . . where no one sees me and where I see no one, but puts me on the proscenium . . . so that everyone sees me and I see everyone.' "[35] As Varlamov so happily recognized, his seat on the proscenium was a crucial step toward uniting stage and auditorium and bringing the theater "out of the stifling narrow theatrical box and into the wide city square,"[36] where the spectators could become part of the "corporate creative art of the performance."[37]

When the audience is viewed as co-creator, it becomes necessary constantly to change the presentation, perhaps with each performance. At least that was the reason Meyerhold liked to give for constantly meddling with his own work. He claimed he once got a letter from a man who had attended twenty performances of one of his productions, only to discover that each show was a "correction" of the one before. The man complained that all performances were essentially unfinished, so why bother to attend a premiere? "But what can we do, comrades?" Meyerhold asked. "Creating a performance is so difficult that it has to be done by all of us together."[38]

Indeed, Meyerhold often held public discussions about his productions after the opening night, and the results of these debates often affected future productions.[39] Perhaps this is what Brecht was referring to in his 1930 notes on the Meyerhold Theater's performance in Berlin, when he wrote that the German critics "refuse to discuss the outcome of many discussions."[40] When it was financially possible, Meyerhold employed people to ask the theatergoers their opinions about a performance and pass around questionnaires.[41]

Questionnaires and public debates notwithstanding, Meyer-

hold even in the post-revolutionary twenties, betrayed a certain
elitist bias, not so different from that of 1909. The audience may
be a co-creator, but there may also be details of a performance
the director will not want to change, no matter what. In such
cases, the director and performers must help the audience understand why such details have to stay. The audience may be
a creative partner, but not necessarily an equal one, and when
it comes to the crunch, the director is still king. Nevertheless,
Meyerhold's efforts to bridge the gap between stage and audience persevered. Seating the elderly Varlamov on the proscenium edge in 1909--a surprising move at the time—was a first
step toward the more radical effects of the twenties, when a
visitor to a Meyerhold production would find that not only did
the stage settings extend into the auditorium, the auditorium
had become part of the setting. For *The Dawns* (1920), the walls
of the theater corridors were lined with posters and slogans,
anticipating the way Falckenberg staged Brecht's *Drums in the
Night* in 1922.

But the closest Meyerhold ever came to having the audience
participate physically in one of his productions was at two performances of *The Dawns*, when there was a stirring though not
entirely spontaneous singing of the "Internationale" by an audience made up largely of Red Army soldiers.[42]

Meyerhold found near at hand a theoretical basis for his stylized theater; others had already prepared the way. A letter from
Leonid Andreev outlined for him the nature of conscious or
stylized theater:

Conscious theater is such, that the spectator never for a minute forgets
that there is before him an actor who is *acting*, and the actor never
forgets that there is in front of him an auditorium, under his feet a
stage, and on each side, scenery. Just as, when looking at a painting,
one never for a minute forgets that here is paint, canvas, brush-strokes,
but nevertheless one gets an enhanced feeling of life. And it is often
thus: the more *painterly*, the stronger the feeling of *life*.[43]

Meyerhold also pointed to statements from Georg Fuchs' *The
Theater of the Future* to support his idea that the usual attempts
at creating illusions are silly and illogical. The audience will

always be required to take imaginative leaps, to accept artifice, no matter how heroic the director's efforts to create illusion.[44]

During his first years as actor and director at the Imperial Theaters in St. Petersburg (from 1908), Meyerhold worked out a theory and practice of the grotesque, a concept which he introduced, as early as 1912, into "the vocabulary of Russian theater."[45] The grotesque, "based on the conflict between content and form," is a means of transcending "the commonplace in life." Because the grotesque emphasizes the outward, visible elements of the production, it tends to promote the development of all those aspects of theater which appeal to the senses: music, dance, movement, gesture. And since the grotesque is itself a synthesis of opposites, it helps us become aware of the paradoxes of life. The "apparently illogical combination of dissimilar elements which comprises the grotesque, by its strangeness helps to avoid sentimentality," and "creates a picture of the objective world which leads the audience toward an attempt to guess at the mystery of the hidden world." When grotesque elements are inserted in a realistic drama (as in *The Unknown Woman*, *Spring's Awakening*, *The Earth Spirit*, *Pandora's Box*, *Vanka the Butler and Jean the Page*), the combination of realism and grotesquerie "compels the audience to have an ambivalent attitude toward what is happening onstage. Isn't it the job of the dramatic grotesque continually to keep the audience in this condition of ambiguity toward the dramatic action, by changing its movement with contrasting strokes?"[46]

This mixture of the fantastic and the realistic which Meyerhold called "the grotesque" is a theatrical expression of the experimentation in montage being carried out by the avant-garde artists Meyerhold knew and worked with.[47] Meyerhold and his colleague Bebutov expressed their kinship with Picasso and Tatlin when they declared that "the contemporary audience wants to see placards, *palpable materials* in the interplay of surfaces and sizes."[48]

In *The Forest* (1924) Meyerhold mixed naturalism and fantasy by presenting a young heroine in natural makeup and ordinary nineteenth-century dress, who meets a young man wearing a green wig and white tennis outfit.[49] The furniture for the play consisted of six ordinary cheap wooden chairs and one chair which was an exact period reproduction. "The single object is thus invested with the concentrated essence of its time and stamps its impression forcibly upon our memories."[50]

Though Meyerhold had begun early in the century to experiment with combinations of realism and abstraction—the "apparently illogical combination of dissimilar elements"—the style was, as late as 1935, a revelation to the American theater scholar Norris Houghton. Houghton spent six months in the Soviet Union that year in order to study Soviet theater. He saw Meyerhold's production of *Camille* and was amazed at the mixture of abstract background and highly realistic furnishings, in particular, the "huge grand piano, Louis XV and XVI chairs, gilt candelabra, fine stuffs strewn about the stage."

All this was far from creating a realistic illusion—there was no doubt that this was complete theatricality—but the surprise at finding Meyerhold using actual things, actual windows and doors and fireplaces at all, was so great that I failed to appreciate just what he was doing with them.

The "wall" of this elegant room was a free-standing panel with a French window in it.[51] This was the sort of effect which Meyerhold in 1909 referred to as a "higher realism," the sort of realism attained by the opera singer Boris Chaliapin, whose art is "always true, not true to life, but true theatrically . . . [and] elevated above life."[52]

Though he was accused of wanting to make actors into puppets, Meyerhold actually followed in the footsteps of his own master, Stanislavsky, for whom the training of young actors was a primary concern.

Always, when I remember the active part which the Art Theater actors had in the creation of the characters and mood of *The Seagull*, I begin to understand how there arose in me my strong belief in the actor as the main element in the theater. It was not the *mise en scène*, not the crickets, not the sound of horses' hoofs on a bridge—none of these created the *mood*; rather, it was the musicality of the actors, who caught the rhythm of Chekhovian poetry.[53]

Meyerhold's rules for the training of actors, set forth in 1907, could have been included in a handbook for actors in Brechtian theater. For instance, the Russian director demanded a cool, emotionally distanced acting style: "Let the new actor express the culmination of the tragic as it was expressed in the sorrow and joy of Mary: with an outward calm, almost *coldly*, without screams and tears, without a shaking voice, but nevertheless deeply."[54] This technique of unemotional acting was effectively summed up by Meyerhold when he admonished his players to "learn from Harold Lloyd, who weeps with vaseline." The Russian director regarded highly emotional acting as "pathological." He saw his actors as "tribunes" and wanted them to remain emotionally distanced so they could impart their own attitudes toward the dramatic events and compel the audience to adopt "a certain attitude."[55] Meyerhold did not deny the emotional side of theater, however. A purely rational theater "would resemble a debating hall. I could read you my speech to the accompaniment of a piano or orchestra . . . but this speech and your presence would not make a performance." It was Meyerhold's opinion that a purely intellectual appeal is against all theatrical "laws" because theater exists for much more than the construction of thesis and antithesis. But the director must do more than acknowledge the audience's emotional needs; he must stimulate and guide these feelings.[56]

Meyerhold's work with opera production inspired another important and fruitful idea—an idea which would become, along with the accusation of puppeteering, forever linked with his name. This was his technique for giving actors a rigorous physical training, so that their whole bodies would be used as sensitive, highly expressive instruments. The method, which he called "biomechanics," consisted of exercises which made possible the exquisitely coordinated choreographies for which his troupe became famous.

Like Gordon Craig, Meyerhold used the puppet in his theoretical writing as a metaphor for the difference between the style of the "new" and the "naturalistic" actor (the latter, being life-like, tries both to experience and to evoke empathy with the role). A marionette is valuable as an entertainer only because and so long as it is doll-like. After all (so Meyerhold's argument runs), a puppet which seems exactly like a human being might as well be replaced by a human actor. Similarly, the actor who tries to pass himself off as a "real-life" character loses his charm as an actor and his value to the theater. In short, an actor should be a creator, not a copier.[57] The acting technique Meyerhold developed was designed to show off the actor's virtuosity as an actor, in contrast to Stanislavsky's method, which aimed to make the actor somehow disappear into his role. In 1912 a critic named Land described the acting style Meyerhold was trying to achieve: "Just as a cardboard silhouette simplifies a portrait, [Meyerhold's] style simplifies acting and psychological portrayal, [even] impoverishes them, but the more schematic these things are, the more well defined [they turn out to be]."[58]

Perhaps one of the most important (and often bitter) lessons Meyerhold learned from his early days at the Art Theater, Komissarzhevskaia's theater, and the Imperial Theaters was that a successful new theater could not come into being unless actors were specially trained intellectually as well as physically to carry out the director's ideas. Because of his interest in training the new actor, Meyerhold always considered the studio an integral part of his theater and constructed for his actors elaborate programs of physical exercise, movement, dance, and acrobatics. The influence of Anna Lacis' teacher, V. M. Bekhterev, is evident in the curriculum of the Meyerhold Studio of 1922–23, where the course of study included "Mimetism and Its Biological Significance (Bekhterev)" and the "Study of Individual and Collective Reflexology." The studio at that time also listed courses in social science, literature, musicology, and the technology of stage production, hardly a curriculum for puppets.[59] A conventionally trained actor who enrolled in the Meyerhold Studio would have to practice nineteenth-century vaudevilles and the techniques of Spanish Golden Age theater, in order to learn their devices.[60] Practice in movement came first, then "thought," and finally training in speech.[61] Meyerhold subscribed to William James' idea that words and emotions arise from certain reflexive movements and cited the following Jamesian example as a rationale for biomechanics: "When we see a bear, we first begin to run, and then, we become frightened because we ran away."[62]

One of Brecht's theories of acting—the art of "double showing" (*das doppelte Zeigen*)—had been pioneered in the Meyerhold Theater of the 1920s. Indeed, one of the most striking elements of a Meyerholdian performance was the degree to which the actors were distanced from their roles. The description Alpers gives of a Meyerholdian "split" performance closely parallels Brecht's essays on the art of the actor and the right relationship between an actor's performance and the audience's reaction to it:

At each moment of the play the actor is divided into the scenic character and the performer who *impersonates* this character before the audience, who makes his own comment upon the character during the perform- ance, who shows him in various attitudes and situations of the scenic performance.

The actor enacts, as it were, not the character itself, but his own attitude to the given character—thus does the Meyerhold theater define the fundamental principle of the actor's craftsmanship. . . .

This splitting up of the art of acting into a character and its com- mentary did not contain anything mystical. It was altogether a ration- alistic art; it laid open before the outsider the very mechanics of the creation of a scenic image.[63]

Meyerhold's model of distanced acting was the actor in Jap- anese *Kabuki* drama who, in intensely emotional moments, ad- dresses the audience something like this: "Attention! A dramatic situation! I very deeply loved my friend; they have slain him, and life will be very hard for me without him. Attention! I will re-enact the scene for you."[64] The actor who portrayed Bruno in *The Magnaminous Cuckold* (1922) performed acrobatic tricks and belched in the middle of pathetic speeches, and generally be- haved in a manner inappropriate to the text. In *The Forest* (1924), while the character Ulita dwells on her romantic fantasies about moonlight nights and the ecstasies of love, the actress portraying Ulita "assumes an obscenely comical posture and sings some old sentimental romance, out of tune." In the same play, love duets were sung while the lovers crawled under the dining- room table.[65]

Meyerhold liked to have his actors do multiple roles, not be- cause there were not enough actors but because the "principle of transformation" is important to a play. It is necessary for the spectators to see these role changes, so they can become aware of the actors' virtuosity.[66] The relationship between actor and role Meyerhold called the actor's "mask." While he tested his players by assigning them a multiplicity of rules, whether in different plays or within a single play (in *Trust D. E.* [1924] the actors had as many as seven different roles in one episode), he nevertheless encouraged them not to fear the repetition of a mask, when that mask turns out to be exactly the right one. Chaplin, for example, was always Chaplin. He used the same makeup, gestures, costume, and other devices, no matter what character he played. Conventional theaters may demand actors who can vanish inside a variety of roles, but that sort of talent, for Meyerhold, was undesirable. He wanted, not the actor's disappearance, but a performer who could let the audience see the player behind the role.[67]

It is a measure of Meyerhold's regard for the actor that he placed so much importance, throughout his career, on stage movement and gesture. Again, the development of his theory and practice in this area began in the early 1910s. For *Sister Beatrice* (1906), Meyerhold for the first time provided each character with his or her own special set of gestures (a kind of physical leit-motif). That same year, in *The Fairground Booth*, each character had unique gestures. He also used gesture to cool down highly emotional scenes as in *Sister Beatrice* and *Hedda Gabler* (1906), where slow, calculated, rhythmical speech and gestures expressed turbulent emotions.[68] For *Hedda Gabler*, Meyerhold used gesture in the wider sense of the expression of inner mental states through use of costume, colors, and static poses. Also in 1906, for his production of Schnitzler's *The Cry of Life*, Meyerhold used "devices of the grotesque" wherever there was great emotional intensity. It was an "experiment in epic-cold narrative."[69]

Meyerhold believed artful movement can help the actor go beyond the text of a play, "to express the inexpressible, to reveal what is hidden." Older theatrical traditions also emphasized movement, but he thought his idea of plasticity added a new element: the actor's movements did not have to conform to his words. Meyerhold pointed out that people often betray their thoughts through movements and gestures, and the thoughts thus revealed may have little or no relationship to what is being said; only through gesture do people disclose their real relationship to each other. Thus two dialogues may be taking place simultaneously: a spoken dialogue and an inner one, the two being quite different, and it is up to the director to show the inner dialogue.[70]

Knowledge of the "science" of stage movement is important not only to director and actors but to the playwright as well. Meyerhold thought playwrights ought to be trained in the science of movement by being required to write pantomimes before they were allowed to write plays with dialogue. The motto for his ideal school for dramatists would have been: "words in the theater are only patterns on the canvas of movement."[71]

This insistence on the primacy of movement in the actor's art was a staple of Meyerhold's system, but the pace changed. The slow, measured pauses and poses of Meyerhold's Symbolist days had, by 1920, speeded up considerably, and the dream-like movements were soon rejected in favor of the dynamism of the Futurists and Constructivists. In 1921, Meyerhold recommended to tired-out Symbolist theaters Marinetti's prescription for rejuvenation:

Replace adultery in the drama with mass scenes;[72] perform the play by beginning at the end of the plot [thus eliminating the expected element of suspense, so bothersome also to Brecht]; utilize for the theater the heroism of the circus and the technology of the machine; spread glue on the spectator's chairs; sell the same ticket to different people; pour out sneezing powder; stage fire and murder in the pit; use the intermission for contests: races around the theater, throwing rings and discus. All for the glory of speed and dynamism.[73]

Meyerhold conceded that on the surface all this is exaggeration, calculated to shock, but insisted there was a more serious purpose to Marinetti's program. The Italian Futurist was trying to free the world from the theater of "half tones, of castrated Lutheranism, of temples draped with cloth, of flabby psychologism."[74]

Perhaps the best example of the new dynamic was in the way Meyerhold staged the lovers' meeting in *The Magnanimous Cuckold*. Ordinarily audiences can expect sweethearts to embrace and kiss when they meet. But Meyerhold's actors communicated their love by a novel series of gestures: the lover climbed to the top of a ten-foot slide, zoomed down (shouting "Wheee!"), and collided with his beloved, knocking her to the floor. So much for "flabby psychologism."

Meyerhold's galvanic theater brought with it a new technology, borrowed from the infant art of filmmaking: the use of film projections onstage. His first use of this device occurred in 1923 in Tretiakov's adaptation of Martinet's *Night* (retitled *The Earth Rampant*). In that production, briefly worded slogans, projected on two screens above the stage, announced the beginning of each episode, indicated its central theme, and emphasized its relevance to current events: DOWN WITH WAR! ATTENTION! THE BLACK INTERNATIONAL. A KNIFE IN THE BACK OF THE REVOLUTION! NIGHT.[75] *The Earth Rampant* projected not only episode titles (the titles themselves were a novelty), but posters with slogans, portraits of revolutionary heroes, and scenes from World War I and the Civil War. For *Trust D. E.* Meyerhold used three projection screens and color transparencies. While documentary material relating to the action onstage was being shown on the two side screens, the middle screen had episode titles which provided information about location and people, commentary on the plot, and excerpts from the writing and speeches of revolutionary leaders.[76]

Piscator used film in a similar manner (for the first time) in his 1924 documentary drama *Flags* and in many of his productions thereafter, including *Rasputin* (1927) and *The Adventures of the Brave Soldier Schwejk* (1927), the latter two being productions in which Brecht had a hand. Thus, Brecht was inaccurate when he claimed that the use of film projections of (Caspar Neher's) drawings for *Mahagonny* (1930) was something new.[77] Brecht again used film projections when he directed *A Man's a Man* in 1931. The films showed Galy Gay before and after each transformation.[78] Pictures flashed on a screen for *The Mother* were evidently very similar to the projections used in *The Earth Rampant* or Piscator's productions of *Flags* and *The Tidal Wave*: scene titles, quotes from Marx and Lenin, photos of historical figures, mottos, emblems such as hammer and sickle, historic events.

Thus while the production per se continued to increase in importance, the text of the play continued to diminish in importance, or rather, the show became the text. From early in his career, Meyerhold insisted on the director's and actor's right to be freed from the author, to interpret a play freely, to decide which stage directions to honor, which to ignore.[79] An essay Meyerhold wrote in 1908 shows that he was already thinking about a new way of staging Gogol's *The Inspector General*. When he did produce that play in 1926, it was with such radical changes in text and interpretation that it became essentially a new play as was the case with another Russian classic, Griboedov's *Woe from Wit* (even the title was changed to *Woe to Wit*). Plans for radically altering *Hamlet* were never realized. He called his ideas about a new presentation of the old repertoire an "echo of times past," which would "provide a thread of continuity from ancient Greek and medieval theater through Shakespeare, Calderón, and Molière, to Russian theater of the 1830s with Gogol at its head, and from Gogol to the present."[80]

Given his cavalier attitude toward the text, it is not surprising that Meyerhold was drawn to *commedia*-style improvisations. He thoughtfully reassured playwrights that they had a place in his theater and that it was not at all degrading for a dramatist to write scenarios for improvisations. They could even write prologues![81]

In defending his adaptation of Verhaeren's *The Dawns*, Meyerhold related his reworking of texts to political circumstances, claiming that wholesale literary adaptation was a necessary outcome of the Revolution, which had changed many things, including popular attitudes toward the classics. The Revolution had made it unnecessary to regard a text as inviolable, because the audience, rather than the text, had become the center of interest. Meyerhold and his co-adaptor Bebutov were severely criticized for altering *The Dawns*, but Meyerhold conceded only that they should have gone much further with their changes and would have done so if they had had more time.[82] It simply made no sense to Meyerhold to remain faithful to texts and stage directions. He was convinced that the old playwrights, if they could return from their graves, would be delighted to find how cleverly their work had been altered to keep pace with modern times. In an interesting parallel with methods used by Brecht and Piscator, Meyerhold in 1920 suggested team adaptation, proposing that the actors, as well as the writers, of a company could be co-adaptors.[83]

Reworking texts is not new, but a conservative tradition has developed. Strong directors such as Meyerhold and Brecht often found it necessary to defend using the text as raw material. The wholesale transferral of an existing text onto the stage, unchanged, represented the sort of slavish "literarization of the theater" which Meyerhold abhorred. His planned repertoire for 1920–21 included works by Shakespeare, Shaw, Mayakovsky, Claudel, and Aristophanes, plays which he referred to as "only literature."

Let [literature] rest quietly in libraries and archives. What we will need are scenarios and we will often make use of even the classics as a canvas for our theatrical creations. The path of reworking we tread without fear, fully convinced of its necessity.[84]

The change in Meyerhold's use of music was in keeping with his move away from the soft melding of artistic elements in Symbolist drama, toward the startling, contrastive separation of artistic elements which characterized his productions from 1917 to the end of his life. From the start, Meyerhold had admired Wagner's concept of the *Gesamtkunstwerk*, the harmonious blending of all the arts. But after the Revolution, he came to believe that in theatrical art, as with the graphic arts, the synthesis must occur in the minds of the spectators. In that way only can they become creative partners. To see how Meyerhold's musical techniques changed, we must look first at the early plays such as *The Death of Tintagiles* (1905), done for the studio of the Moscow Art Theater. That play was accompanied throughout by orchestra and *a cappella* choir; the music harmonized with, and intensified, the "mood." When the curtain rose for the third act of *Schluck and Jau*, one could hear a duet in the style of the eighteenth century. The audience saw the princess and her ladies-in-waiting seated in a series of garden arbors, embroidering, raising and lowering their embroidery needles exactly in time with each other and with the music. Indeed, everything in the play was done in a harmonious musical rhythm: "movements, gestures, words, the colors of the settings and costumes." In the studio's version of Maeterlinck's *Seven Princesses*, "the dialogue was always spoken against a background of music, drawing the spirit of the audience into the world of Maeterlinckian drama."[85] But for *The Earth Rampant* music was used in quite a different way. The traditionally hidden musicians were moved right onto the stage, in full view of the audience. Their music provided an ironic commentary on the action, especially when a chamber pot was brought onstage for the "Tsar" who used it to the accompaniment of "God Save the Tsar." *Trust D. E.* had a jazz band seated onstage; it was the first public jazz performance in the Soviet Union. The onstage orchestra was a device Brecht used in 1928 in *The Threepenny Opera* and again in 1949 in *Mother Courage*. For his production of Faiko's *Teacher Bubus* (1924), Meyerhold also contrasted music with text. He described the production as being carried out on two levels. On one level was the music, on the other, the action onstage. When the acting was quiet and peaceful, the music showed excitement, and vice versa. The music of Chopin and Liszt and jazz were used, perhaps in a manner similar to *The Resistible Rise of Arturo Ui* (written 1941, premiered 1958), in which Brecht's directions called for Chopin's "Funeral March" to be played as dance music. The purpose of the contrastive use of music in *Teacher Bubus* was to keep the audience in a state of tension, and to transfer the emotional tension away from the actor and dialogue to the music.[86]

In one crucial way, however, Meyerhold's use of music did not change over the years. He always kept his vision of the dramatic production as an essentially symphonic work in which all elements of the show—actors, words, groupings, colors, costumes—form an unheard but exquisitely orchestrated piece of music.

By 1924 Meyerhold's achievements were the most important part of the theatrical news which came out of the Soviet Union. When the various artists, intellectuals, and "cultural ambassadors" Brecht knew, spoke or wrote about Meyerhold, they would have described a director who had turned from the slow dark mysticism of Symbolist theater toward "light, joy, spaciousness and easy creativity," and who had, years before, declared his intention to make the audience a truly creative partner.[87]

NOTES

1. Brecht's first attempt at directing occurred in 1922, with his friend Arnolt Bronnen's *Vatermord* (*Patricide*), but he was replaced as director shortly before the play was staged.

2. Konstantin Rudnitsky points out, in *Meyerhold the Director*, ed. Sydney Schultze (Ann Arbor, Mich.: Ardis, 1921), p. 129, that Meyerhold, having laid the groundwork for Symbolist theater, quickly moved on to other forms, while directors such as Stanislavsky and Nemirovich-Danchenko continued to labor in that field.

3. For an informative essay on Symbolist theater, see Daniel Gerould's "Russian Symbolist Drama and the Visual Arts," *Newsnotes on Soviet and East European Drama and Theatre*, 4 (March 1984): 10–17.

4. Rudnitsky, *Meyerhold the Director*, p. 56.

5. Ibid., p. 106.

6. Ibid., p. 65–66.

7. In working with his set designers, Brecht liked to combine model building and impressionist sketches. For example, in his work with Karl von Appen on *The Caucasian Chalk Circle*, Brecht had von Appen first create a series of sketches; then models were constructed from the sketches. However, both models and sketches were subject to constant alteration and were used as Meyerhold used his designs, for their suggestive power rather than as patterns set in concrete. See Karl von Appen, "Über das Bühnenbild," in W. Hecht, ed., *Materialien zu Brechts "Der Kaukasische Kreidekreis"* (Frankfurt a.M.: Suhrkamp, 1968), p. 96–98. Meyerhold continued to work with models, perhaps the most notable one being El Lissitsky's Constructivist setting for Tretiakov's *I Want a Baby*.

8. *Stat'i, Pis'ma, Rechi, Besedy*, 1:109.

9. Edward Braun, ed. and trans., *Meyerhold on Theatre* (New York: Hill and Wang, 1969), pp. 282–83.

10. Rudnitsky, *Meyerhold the Director*, p. 79.

11. Ibid., pp. 125–26.

12. Alexander Bakshy, *The Path of the Modern Russian Stage and Other Essays* (London: Palmer & Hayward, 1916), p. 76.

13. *SPRB* 1 (1907): 250. This device of the intruding author would reappear in the twenties with Meyerhold's suggestion that during the performance of *I Want a Baby*, Tretiakov might walk onstage from time to time to instruct or correct the actors. See Fevral'skii, "S. M. Tret'iakov," in S. Tret'iakov, *Slyshish', Moskva?!*, pp. 200–202.

14. Boris Alpers, *The Theatre of the Social Mask*, trans. Mark Schmidt (New York: Group Theatre, Inc., 1934), p. 48.

15. Braun, *Meyerhold on Theatre*, p. 21.

16. Boris Singermann, "Brechts *Dreigroschenoper*. Zur Ästhetik der Montage," *Brecht-Jahrbuch* 1976, ed. John Fuegi et al. (Frankfurt a.M.: Suhrkamp, 1976): 73.

17. *SPRB* 1: 255.

18. Braun, *Meyerhold on Theatre*, p. 116.

19. Nikolai Gorchakov, *The Theater in Soviet Russia*, trans. Edgar Lehrman (New York: Columbia University Press, 1957), p. 62; André von Gyseghem, *Theatre in Soviet Russia* (London: Faber and Faber, 1943), pp. 18–19.

20. Norris Houghton, *Moscow Rehearsals*, 2d ed. (New York: Grove Press, 1962), p. 18.

21. Braun, *Meyerhold on Theatre*, p. 22.

22. *SPRB* 1 (1907): 251.

23. *SPRB* 1: 160.

24. "The literary critic Immermann has remained up to the present practically undiscovered," according to Benno von Wiese, *Karl Immermann* (Bad Homburg: Verlag Dr. Max Gehlen, 1969), p. 125. The fact that Meyerhold knew of Immermann's work is further evidence of the depth and breadth of the Russian director's reading and general knowledge of Western thought and culture.

25. *SPRB* 1 (1909): 160.

26. *SPRB* 1: 254–55.

27. *SPRB* 1: 254.

28. *SPRB* 2 (1929–30): 194.

29. Houghton, *Moscow Researsals*, p. 105. Here, Houghton is describing Meyerhold's production of *Camille*.

30. *SPRB* 1: 245; Mark Slonim, *Russian Theater* (New York: World, 1961), p. 192.

31. Erast Garin, *S Meierkhol'dom: Vospominaniia* (Moscow: Iskusstvo, 1974), p. 221.

32. See the photographs in Julius Bab, *Das Theater der Gegenwart. Geschichte der dramatischen Bühne seit 1870* (Leipzig: Verlagsbuchhandlung von J. J. Weber, 1928), pp. 181–83, 189, 190–93, 220–21. Pages 192–93, 218–19 deal at length with the influence of Russian theater (in particular Constructivist and Cubist styles) on German avant-garde theater. Piscator used a global setting for his production of Alexei Tolstoy's *Rasputin* (1927); Brecht, as part of Piscator's writers' collective, helped revise the script. Piscator's staging of Ernst Toller's *Hooray, We're Alive* (*Hoppla, wir leben*, 1927) had a Constructivist-style set.

33. Vsevolod Meierkhol'd, *Perepiska* (Moscow: Iskusstvo, 1976), pp. 29–30.

34. *SPRB* 1 (1909): 175–78.

35. Rudnitsky, *Meyerhold the Director*, p. 152.

36. *SPRB* 2 (1920): 483–84.

37. *SPRB* 2 (1920): 483.

38. *SPRB* 2 (1927): 159.

39. Rosemarie Tietze, "Das Neue Theater. Meyerhold 1917 bis 1930," in R. Tietze, ed., *Vsevolod Meyerhold: Theaterarbeit 1917–1930* (Munich: Carl Hanser, 1974), p. 36.

40. *Schriften zum Theater* 1 (April 1930), 234–35.

41. Tietze, *Meyerhold*, p. 36. For Meyerhold's further comments on the idea of the audience as co-creator, see *SPRB* 2 (1921–22): 43; (1929–30): 96, 195. A report from the Soviet Union by Federal Theatre Project Director Hallie Flanagan ("Ivan as Critic," *Theatre Guild Magazine*, 4 [January 1930]: 40–42) indicated that polling the audience was mandatory and not unique to Meyerhold's theater. In this very interesting article, Flanagan described the method used to objectively analyze audience reaction:

Nightly in these theatres where youth is instructing age, the audience is closely studied. At each premiere, observers appointed by the central committee watch the spectators for reactions. The play is divided into moments and the mood of the audience for each moment is tabulated. *Roar, China!*, for instance, has 507 moments. The reaction of each, as evidenced by attention, applause, laughter, tears, hisses, is recorded. The result is drawn up in the form of a chart sent to the producer, and in the light of the evidence the directors and actors make such changes as they think best.

Flanagan also described the second method of recording audience reaction, the distribution of questionnaires, "an assistant helping those who cannot read or write." The questionnaire, which began by commanding " 'Citizens! Answer the given question! Doing so you help build the new theater,' " demanded such information as " 'What sort of play do you want to see during the next season? Tragedy, melodrama, farce, comedy, revue.' "

42. Marjorie L. Hoover, *Meyerhold: The Art of Conscious Theater* (Amherst, Mass.: University of Massachusetts Press, 1974), pp. 92–93.

43. *SPRB* 1 (1907): 141–42.

44. *SPRB* 1 (1906): 121.

45. Rudnitsky, *Meyerhold the Director*, p. 160.

46. *SPRB* 1 (1912): 224–29. Meyerhold's concept of the grotesque is analyzed at length in Christian Mailand-Hansen, *Mejerchol'ds Theater-*

ästhetik in den 1920er Jahren (Copenhagen: Rosenkilde und Bagger, 1980), pp. 193–95.

47. Boris Zingerman has written about the montage style of Brecht's *The Threepenny Opera* (1928) and the relationship of this style to circus and music hall performances, as well as to Cubist painting, jazz, and Eisenstein's theories, observing that "the basic principle of this sort of dramatic construction was originally developed by Meyerhold." Singermann, *Brecht-Jahrbuch*, 1976: 71.

48. *SPRB* 2 (1920): 16. Tatlin's "painting reliefs," made of tin, wood, glass, and plaster, which he began constructing in 1913, were, like Meyerhold's theatrical work, an attempt to reach out to the audience.

49. There is an anecdote that shortly after the premiere, someone asked Meyerhold the reason for the green wig, and, not being able to remember the reason, he had the actor discard the wig, and it appeared no more in the performances.

50. van Gyseghem, *Theater in Soviet Russia*, p. 19.

51. Houghton, *Moscow Rehearsals*, pp. 18–19.

52. *SPRB* 1: 144.

53. *SPRB* 1 (1906): 122.

54. *SPRB* 1: 134. These words bring to mind a scene in Brecht's production of *Mother Courage* (1949) in which Helene Weigel in the title role calmly denied knowing her own dead son and then, when the soldiers had gone, expressed her agony in a silent scream.

55. *SPRB* 2 (1925): 92, 94.

56. *SPRB* 2 (1929–30): 192–93.

57. *SPRB* 1 (1912): 215–16.

58. *SPRB* 1 (c. 1912): 247.

59. Hoover, *Meyerhold*, pp. 311–19.

60. Braun, *Meyerhold on Theatre*, p. 146.

61. *SPRB* 2 (1930): 239.

62. *SPRB* 2 (1925): 92, 534.

63. Boris Alpers, *The Theatre of the Social Mask*, trans. Mark Schmidt (New York: Group Theater, 1934), pp. 36–37.

64. *SPRB* 2 (1931): 246.

65. Alpers, *The Theatre of the Social Mask*, pp. 36–37.

66. *SPRB* 2 (1924): 62.

67. *SPRB* 2 (1925): 75.

68. *SPRB* 1 (1912): 248.

69. *SPRB* 1 (c. 1912): 244.

70. *SPRB* 1 (1907): 135.

71. *SPRB* 1 (1912): 211–12. Blok's reaction to that dictum was "Oh my God!" (Rudnitsky, *Meyerhold the Director*, p. 198).

72. Brecht expressed essentially the same idea when he wrote in 1930 that groups, not individuals, must be the focal point of the new drama (*SzT* 1: 258).

73. *SPRB* 2 (1921): 28–29 (written with V. Bebutov and K. Derzhavin). Filippo Tommaso Marinetti (1876–1944) was an Italian writer and theoretician of Futurism.

74. *SPRB* 2 (1921): 28–29.

75. Braun, *The Theatre of Meyerhold*, p. 180. Braun rightly observes that "Both in its form and objectives, Tretyakov's treatment [of Martinet's play] closely resembled what Brecht was later to call 'Epic.' "

76. Tietze, "Theater," p. 16; Herbert Marshall, *The Pictorial History of the Russian Theatre* (New York: Crown, 1977), p. 132.

77. *SzT* 2 (1930): 119–20.

78. *SzT* 2 (1931): 71–72.

79. *SPRB* 1: 238–39; Braun, *The Theatre of Meyerhold*, p. 95.

80. *SPRB* 1 (1908): 172–73.

81. *SPRB* 1 (1912): 214–15. In collaboration with two others, Meyerhold wrote a scenario adaptation of Gozzi's *The Love of Three Oranges* (1761), which was published in the journal of the Meyerhold Studio in 1913 and inspired Prokofiev's opera.

82. *SPRB* 2 (1920): 17.

83. *SPRB* 2 (1920): 483.

84. *SPRB* 2 (1920): 483.

85. *SPRB* 1: 110, 244.

86. *SPRB* 2 (1925): 83, 85.

87. *SPRB* 2 (1920): 483.

1. Portrait of Vsevolod Meyerhold. [Billy Rose Theatre Collection. The New York Public Library at Lincoln Center. Astor, Lenox and Tilden Foundations]

2. Bertolt Brecht. [German Information Center]

3. A scene from Meyerhold's production of *Roar, China!* (1926), by Sergei Tretiakov. Realistically dressed coolies pull their heavy load in front of an abstract setting. [Billy Rose Theatre Collection. The New York Public Library at Lincoln Center. Astor, Lenox and Tilden Foundations]

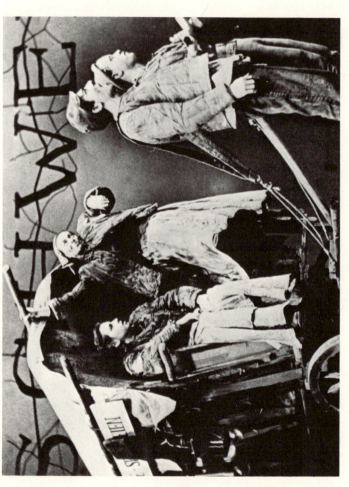

4. A scene from Brecht's production of *Mother Courage and Her Children* (1953). Realistically dressed peasants pull their heavy load in front of an abstract setting. Helene Weigel as Mother Courage, Angelika Hurwicz as Kattrin, Ernst Kahler as Eilif, and Hannes Fischer as Schweizerkas. [German Information Center]

5. Meyerhold's *Woe to Wit* (1928), by Aleksandr Griboedov. The Dining Room Episode. [Edward Braun]

6. Brecht's production of *Herr Puntila and His Man Matti* (1948). The Dining Room Episode. [Deutsches Theatermuseum, Munich]

7. Two doomed wise men: Azdak (played by Ernst Busch) in Brecht's production of *The Caucasian Chalk Circle* (1954) [William Seymour Theatre Collection, Princeton University Library] and *(overleaf)* Sergei Tretiakov, 1927.

Sergei Tretiakov, 1927. [Portrait by Aleksandr Rodchenko. Phillipe Sers, éditeur]

3

"THE ACTORS WERE SERVED UP IN PORTIONS ON SMALL PLATFORM-PLATES"

Brecht is famous for, among other things, his montage productions. His first truly montage play premiered in 1928 when he and Weill presented the sensationally popular *Threepenny Opera*. Some two years earlier, during the 1926–27 season, Walter Benjamin, visiting Moscow a second time, saw three Meyerhold productions done in the montage style: *Trust D. E.*, with its exuberant agitprop message and physical dynamism; *The Forest*, mixing Constructivist abstraction and real objects; and *The Inspector General*, with its somber, almost Symbolist tableaux.

Trust D. E. was a political revue which, by using moving "walls," three film screens, projected captions, and spotlights, imitated the fast movement and quick scene change of cinema. Benjamin may very well have talked to Brecht about this production, how Meyerhold boldly seated his musicians right on stage, in full view of the audience, and how he aggressively showed off his actors' quick-change virtuosity (ninety-five roles were performed by forty-four actors).[1]

The Forest was Meyerhold's first great venture in remaking a classic text into political theater. Here also the director continued his work with text fragmentation; the original five acts were eventually broken up into thirty-three episodes (in 1926, however, Benjamin probably saw either a sixteen- or twenty-six-episode version).[2] Though frowned on by official arbiters of public taste, this radical fragmentation was evidently well received by audiences, since (according to Rudnitsky) the device was widely copied by other Soviet theaters. Class distinctions were made obvious through exaggerated, grotesque outward appearances (as Brecht was to do several years later in *Mann ist Mann*, *The Roundheads and the Peakheads*, and *The Caucasian Chalk Circle*). The scenic juxtaposition of a large Constructivist bridge with a multitude of real objects intensified the montage style, as did the jarring combination of political propaganda, circus atmosphere, abstraction, realism, vulgarity, and romantic lyricism. The controversy surrounding *Trust D. E.* and *The Forest* had already died down somewhat by the time Benjamin arrived in Moscow, both plays having premiered two years before, in 1924.

Such was not the case with Meyerhold's version of *The Inspector General*. The critics were still yowling when Lacis and Reich took their friend Benjamin to see it. Again a classic text was revised, and radically so. This was not the great masterpiece with which Russian audiences had grown comfortable over the past century. This was a new, Gogol-Meyerhold production: a tragicomedy instead of what had always been interpreted as farce.

The plot is Gogol's. A small-town mayor informs his brother officials of the imminent arrival of an Inspector from St. Petersburg, supposedly travelling incognito.[3] They fear such a visit because they are thoroughly corrupt, governing the town strictly for their own profit. Unfortunately for them, they mistake for the dread Inspector a destitute ne'er-do-well stranger named Khlestakov who, being unscrupulous himself, sets about gleaning all possible advantage from the officials' mistake. He encourages the advances of the mayor's wife, while promising to marry the mayor's daughter, all the time being wined, dined, and bribed by the frightened bureaucrats. In the end they are first shocked to learn the truth about Khlestakov, who has handily skipped town, and then benumbed by the announcement that the real Inspector has arrived.

Gogol wrote the first draft of the play in 1835; it staged the following year. This production, which set the tone for most of the later versions, was done as a farce, to Gogol's great distress.

The sharp edges of satire were washed away by the actors' light-comedy style and by the audience's light-hearted response. So Meyerhold set out to restore and enlarge upon Gogol's original intention. The result was a serious satire of human lust, greed, and cowardice, of the outward beauty and luxury which mask corruption, and of a social-political system which both nourishes and feeds on such foulness.

Paradoxically, Meyerhold began by recovering certain farcical elements from the first draft (which Gogol, hoping to force a more serious reading of his play, had eliminated from the canonical edition of 1842). Meyerhold also added characters and dialogue which were drawn partly from his own imagination and partly from Gogol's other works, including letters and essays. In order to help counteract the farcical interpretation, to lend the play "authenticity and significance," and to make room for his own contributions, Meyerhold greatly lengthened the play and slowed its tempo. The original probably ran no longer than two hours; Meyerhold's version lasted about four hours. Gogol's five-act play was divided by Meyerhold into fifteen titled episodes, with, besides the new characters and new dialogue, a wealth of new stage "business": gestures, movements, poses, and pauses.

The most interesting changes occurred in the central character. Despite his argument that the changes made in *The Inspector General* brought the play closer to Gogol's original intentions, Meyerhold's conception of Khlestakov was quite different from the author's. Gogol had described Khlestakov as "not a professional fraud or deliberate impostor," but one who "almost believes his own words" and "does not lie coldly and deliberately, but theatrically and passionately."[4] Meyerhold's Khlestakov, on the other hand, was a calculating liar and a downright sinister character besides. In the "classic" 1921 Moscow Art Theater production (directed by Stanislavsky, with Mikhail Chekhov in the leading role), Khlestakov had been portrayed as a naive, childlike man who, having by chance been mistaken for an important official, almost helplessly enjoys the benefits of this error. The tremendous difference between Stanislavsky's and Meyerhold's vision of Khlestakov was obvious to the audience the moment Erast Garin first appeared onstage. Where Mikhail

Chekhov had shown in his Khlestakov a man physically dev-
astated by hunger, almost too weak to stand, Garin presented
hunger of a different sort: the audience saw an energetic con-
fidence man, whistling a tune. He was oddly dressed in a costume which made him appear both comic and sinister: top hat,
dark frock coat, a plaid shawl draped across one shoulder, a
bagel suspended from his lapel, dark gloves, a slicked-down
Napoleonic hairdo, and square spectacles with heavy dark rims
which dominated the pale, narrow face. Garin's Khlestakov was
"evilly hungry": the emptiness of his belly was the physical
representation of an awesome moral emptiness.[5]

Meyerhold made Khlestakov's soliloquies into dialogue by
adding a mysterious "travelling officer" as Khlestakov's constant
companion and confidant. Although Meyerhold always main-
tained that the "travelling officer" was inserted for purely technical reasons (to avoid soliloquies), it was only natural for those
who saw the play to assume that this new character represented
a mystical alter-ego or double for Khlestakov.

The sexual implications in Gogol's play were emphasized by
the voluptuous costuming, makeup, and lascivious behavior of
the mayor's wife (played by Meyerhold's beloved second wife,
Zinaida Raikh) as well as by the addition of certain episodes,
such as the one in which Bobchinsky suddenly emerges from a
wardrobe, where he has been watching the mayor's wife un-
dress. Gogol's stage direction that the mayor's wife and daughter
wear four different costumes during the course of the play became four onstage undressing scenes. The director also added
a scene in which Khlestakov, dancing a quadrille, leeringly courts
both wife and daughter. The sexual fantasies of the mayor's wife
were embodied in the sudden appearance of a number of hand-
some young officers who literally crawl out of the woodwork.
They offer her flowers, serenade her, faint, and even die for
love of her.

Meyerhold fragmented *The Inspector General* as he had *The
Forest*, but in another respect he made a surprising departure
from his own recent productions. The stage spaces which had
been opened up in his latest shows were now compressed and
crowded, as in his 1917 production of Lermontov's *Masquerade*.
For *The Inspector General*, numerous actors and gorgeous, pon-

derous period furnishings were squeezed onto small movable platforms which Meyerhold himself had designed.[6] Brecht's use of the crowded setting device in *The Caucasian Chalk Circle*, though inspired by Breughel's painting "The Peasant Wedding," might also owe something to the packed platforms of *The Inspector General*. As in *The Caucasian Chalk Circle*, the crowdedness heightened the comedy and gave each scene the feel of a painting suddenly come to life. Each set seemed to be an exact period reproduction, but there was subtle grotesquerie throughout, and no inward psychological probing. Even the characters' fantasies were given physical shape.

Although the costumes and settings for *The Inspector General* seemed (at first glance) historically accurate, Meyerhold had not by any means abandoned his commitment to the dramatic power of evocation. In 1926 he was as deeply committed to the principle of suggestion through psychological association as he had been in 1906. The actor, director, stage designer, and playwright were still, in Meyerhold's practice, to provide only the key parts, the essences of a place or idea, and the audience as creative co-worker still had to provide the rest, through psychological interaction with the artistic material. For *The Inspector General*, Meyerhold's goal was to evoke the spirit of Nicholas I's Russia, rather than to present a museum-like reproduction of that time and place. The darkly gleaming mahogany-like panels which surrounded the acting area were supposed to suggest the comfortable bourgeois life of the 1830s and 1840s.[7] These screens were used as background to frame the brightly colored, luxuriantly "real" objects in front of them (elegant furniture, bowls of fruit, and so on), and were arranged in a half-circle on the stage so that most episodes used less than the full stage area. The screen at the center back, which had three doors, opened like a gate. During the course of the play trapezoidal platforms on rails with crowded settings and actors already in place were rolled forward toward the audience. All but four of the fifteen episodes were enacted on these small (approximately 14 feet by 12 feet) platforms, thus intensifying the claustrophobic atmosphere of the screened-off space. Each platform was tilted slightly toward the audience, creating the effect of a reversed perspective; actors who stood at the back appeared taller than those at the front. As each episode finished, the platform rolled back behind the center screen. This was the basic design. The platform sets were characterized by a luxurious semirealism: elegant period furnishings, gleaming wood tables upon which were piled real fruit, real food, and drink. Everything reflected the opulent life of the prosperous bourgeoisie, but it was far from being a faithful imitation of the past. Rather, there was exaggeration everywhere.[8] This contrapuntal presentation of the realistic and the fantastic occurred in every aspect of the staging of *The Inspector General*, from the contrast between the paneled outer setting and the hyper-realistic inner setting, to the bodying forth of the characters' fantasies, as though the fantasy were reality.

To see the fantastic in the real world does not mean, as many critics claim, that one is a mystic. It means, rather, to push aside the boundaries of everyday life and plunge into that joy of being which springs forth only in the real world.[9]

Around 1925, a new word (though not a new concept) began to appear in Meyerhold's theoretical vocabulary: "pre-acting." Pre-acting referred to the system of gestures which precede the words in a text. For example, an actor onstage opens a telegram. At first the audience cannot wait to find out what the message is. But the actor, through pre-acting, transfers audience attention from the content of the telegram to his own acting technique. The spectators become interested, not in *what* the telegram says, but in *how* the actor expresses his feelings about it. Through pre-acting, the Meyerholdian actor was expected to reveal to the audience the very roots of the playwright's words. The actor-tribune (as Meyerhold styled his performers) "enacts not only the situation, but its inner kernel." Not only must the actor show the hidden social origins of the dialogue, but also his own purpose in making the revelation! Exactness was considered one of the most crucial elements in pre-acting. Each gesture needs to be, Meyerhold insisted, as thoughtfully chosen as any other element of the production.[10]

In *The Inspector General*, pre-acting, gesture, and careful groupings of actors were used to convey certain themes and motifs. One episode found the hero Khlestakov lolling grandly on the mayor's divan, with his host's beautiful wife and daughter seated next to him, while the mayor and other officials were all respectfully standing.

Khlestakov: Sirs, why are we standing? (He jumps to his feet and with a commanding gesture insists on his invitation.) Please, sit down!

Official: It is customary to stand up for awhile.

Khlestakov: Don't stand on ceremony, I beg you to sit down!

At this juncture, Meyerhold had the mayor and officials obediently lower their behinds into empty space and remain in this posture for the rest of the episode. Through such devices of grouping and posing actors Meyerhold contrasted "the cowardice of the officials and the boldness of the women," a contrast which he saw as one of the important motifs of the play.[11]

Despite the controversy it stirred, *The Inspector General* at least was staged and theatergoers were free to accept or reject it. Such was not the case with Tretiakov's *I Want a Baby.* In December 1929, to a closed session of Glavrepertkom (the censorship department), Meyerhold presented a plan for staging the play as debate drama. Some years later Meyerhold argued that the purpose of theater was not to present solutions, but to show problems so clearly that the audience, after seeing the performance, would think about the issues.[12]

Tretiakov, too, wanted to incorporate "healthy public debate" right into the body of the play. He planned to extend the auditorium up to and even onto the stage, from which vantage point a panel of representatives from various social organizations could interrupt the action in order to discuss key issues as they were raised. Actors and play would serve as outline for the discussants; the theater would become a kind of operating room, a place to observe and dissect.[13] Meyerhold and Tretiakov tried in vain—for four years—to get *I Want a Baby* past the censor. Had they succeeded, it would have been Meyerhold's most radical attempt to create a rational theater and to blur the distinction between audience and performance.

It is interesting to compare the differing visions of the audience in *I Want a Baby* and Meyerhold's 1930 production of Mayakovsky's *The Bathhouse* (which, though permitted, received very hostile reviews). In *I Want a Baby*, the audience is treated as a highly respected co-creator of the drama. Non-actors were to sit onstage and express serious opinions about the highly controversial content of the play. Perhaps this show represented the last gasp of that social idealism which caused Meyerhold to join the Bolsheviks so unhesitatingly in 1917. The "audience" of *The Bathhouse*, in contrast, are cartoon characters—on one level, wonderfully funny, but viciously coarse and stupid nonetheless. They kill theater, rather than help create it. *The Bathhouse* opened on March 16, 1930; hostile reviews were published even before the premiere.[14] A few months later, Mayakovsky was dead, apparently a suicide.

In the third act of *The Bathhouse* the stage includes the orchestra seats, with actors occupying them as though they were part of the real audience watching the play. "The audience looks at the stage through opera glasses, and the [actors on] stage look at the audience through opera glasses."[15] The bureaucrat Pobedonosikov and his flunkies enter and take their seats among the "audience." The "Director" of the play emerges and anxiously questions Pobedonosikov about his reaction to Acts I and II. Because Pobedonosikov is an important official with "connections," the Director is eager to secure his approval of the production. Unfortunately, Pobedonosikov heartily dislikes the play; he is offended by the portrayal of himself, bored with the Director's premise that theater should have an intellectually galvanizing effect on the audience, and disappointed that the Director has avoided a realistic style.

Pobed: It's all laid on too thick. Life isn't like that. . . . Take, for instance, that Pobedonosikov. Whatever you say, it's unseemly.[. . .] We don't have officials like that. It's unnatural. Not lifelike. Not the way things are. You'll have to rewrite that part—tone it down, poeticize it, soften the contours. . . .

Director: . . . our idea was to put the theater into the service of the struggle and positive action. People look, and they get to work. They look, and they are aroused. They look, and they expose whatever is bad.

Pobed: For my part, I'm asking you, in the name of all workers and peasants, not to arouse *me*! Think it over, you alarm clock! Instead of arousing me, you should create pleasant sights and sounds for my eyes and ears.[...] You must go back to the classics! You must learn from the great geniuses of the damn past!

Act 3, The Bathhouse

Under pressure from Pobedonosikov and the social forces he represents, the Director denies his own artistic integrity in order to toady to the philistine's taste. For his pleasure the Director presents an impromptu allegorical ballet representing the triumph of world Communism. This ballet, the incarnation of Pobedonosikov's idea of art, is staggering in its display of unembarrassed *kitsch*. But it makes the bureaucrat and his friends happy. He hurries from the theater as soon as the ballet is over, remarking, "What we just saw is real art. It makes sense to me, to Ivan Ivanovich, [Pobedonosikov's flunky] and to the masses." Pobedonosikov exits from the play-within-a-play only to reenter the "bathhouse" of Mayakovsky's satire.

Given the difficulties Meyerhold was experiencing in staging the work of contemporary playwrights (his attempted production of Erdman's *The Suicide* was banned in 1932), it is not surprising that he practically gave up the attempt in favor of reworking classic dramas (an old specialty of his anyway). But he had to justify, esthetically and ideologically, making political theater from plays which influential critics regarded as inviolable. By the mid-1930s, Meyerhold had developed, perhaps from sheer necessity, what might be called an esthetic of adaptation. It ran like this: all art has its political side and can never be separated from politics, because art reflects the class divisions of society. Therefore, when one remakes a play, one should try to retain its essence—that which makes it a classic—while emphasizing the political and social elements (which have always been there but may not previously have been so obvious to the audience).[16] The director-adaptor should retain the "basic idea" (or "basic ideology") of the author, but has the privilege of deciding just what the basic idea is.[17]

In Meyerhold's various writings about adaptation, the text itself often takes second place to the director's "rights." Meyerhold held that the greater the writer, the more varied and numerous are the possible interpretations of the text. He offered as an example his own ideas about a production of *Hamlet*, in which Hamlet would be portrayed by two actors (onstage at the same time), one commenting on the other's speeches.[18] Despite his readiness, even eagerness, to change a playwright's work, Meyerhold was careful to point out that it is not always necessary to change the text of a play in order to present it in a fresh light. An unusual casting choice, a skillful actor's interpretation of a role can make many an old vehicle suddenly new and strange.[19]

But the "path of reworking" could not save Meyerhold or his theater. In 1936 he planned two major productions as radical adaptations of classic texts: Pushkin's *Boris Godunov* and Mayakovsky's *The Bedbug* (considered a modern classic since December 1935, when Stalin announced that "Mayakovsky was and remains the best, the most talented poet of our Soviet era"[20]). For *Boris Godunov*, Meyerhold decided to go "back to the program which Pushkin outlined and which he could not fulfill because of the technical situation of the time." Following a strategy similar to the one he used with *The Inspector General*, Meyerhold planned to use material from Pushkin's letters, journal articles, and notes Pushkin himself had written on the play.[21]

Meyerhold's *Boris Godunov* (with music by Prokofiev) might have been his greatest masterpiece, even surpassing *The Inspector General*. But it became too big for his little theater, and he had to put the project aside until he could present it at the new and radically designed theater which was being built to his specifications. He was murdered, however, before the theater was completed.

In 1936 Meyerhold's reworking of *The Bedbug* was begun with much optimism and energy. True to his and Mayakovsky's principles, Meyerhold planned to change the text in order to keep it historically up to date and give the audience a greater feeling of personal involvement, in a manner reminiscent of the schemes for audience participation in *I Want a Baby*. The strategy for adapting *The Bedbug* was much the same as that used for *The Inspector General* and *Boris Godunov*. Meyerhold planned to use elements from the whole corpus of the author's work, envisioning this production as "only the first step toward the dramatic consolidation of the literary legacy of the poet."[22] But 1936 was not a good year for Meyerhold; virulent attacks against him were mounting. (Meyerholdism had become a synonym for Formalism.) It was no time to meddle with the literary legacy of Mayakovsky, whose reputation was just then being "propagated like potatoes in the time of Catherine the Great" by the Soviet regime. The new version of *The Bedbug* was never staged.

Although his use of instrumental music changed from the 1910s (music complements and heightens the play's "mood") to the 1920s and 1930s (music stands apart from and comments on the action), Meyerhold's conception of music in drama always went far beyond the merely audible. He envisioned each of his productions as a musical creation, because every part of the production—actors, settings, colors, movement—was one element in the larger rhythmic composition. Music in the literal sense of an arrangement of tones was an important part of this composition and was used in a variety of ways, but Meyerhold would have regarded his work as "musical" even if no musicians or singers had taken part. (He had been aware, from his Moscow Art Theater days, of the formal musicality of Chekhov's drama.) He praised *The Bedbug* for its musical structure, comparing it to a Hindemith quartet. By daring to deviate from the rules of classical music, Hindemith, like Mayakovsky, had created his own artistic rules and taught the audience to accept them. According to Meyerhold, Mayakovsky never intended the second act of his play (set in 1979) as a portrayal of the future. Act II, and the play as a whole, was meant to satirize the time in which it was written—the Soviet Union of the twenties. *The Bedbug* attacked contemporary society in two quite different styles: Act I with gaudy settings and comic-strip characters who behave in the clownish manner of vaudeville performers, and Act II with geometrical forms and cool colors. Social satire becomes, as in music, a theme with variations, and the motif which unites the two movements is the figure of Prisypkin, the funny-pitiful clown.

For Meyerhold, music was also an indispensable device for encouraging audience creativity. From the 1910s, he had been fascinated by the theatrical possibilites of the Wagnerian leitmotif, a form of musical pre-acting which fires certain mental associations in the spectators' minds, drawing them into the creative process.[23] Meyerhold also liked the "broiling" music of classic Japanese and Chinese theater, whose flutes and drums, "sibilant and piping instruments," encouraged playgoers' creativity by at least keeping them awake.[24]

The political-artistic reaction that began in earnest in Russia around 1930 made it necessary for Meyerhold to spend much time and energy defending various aspects of the anti-illusionistic theater he had begun to develop nearly thirty years before: it is not art's business to recreate life, he argued; the theater is, by its very nature, stylized, as is all art. Art is not the realistic wax figure but the unlifelike marble statue; a real nose on a portrait and the portrait looks silly. As Brecht would do some twenty years later, Meyerhold attempted to placate his critics by trying to persuade them that his stylized theater represented an essential "realism." "But within the framework of stylized theater we are profound realists. We try to create realistic characters. . . . We are speaking of stylized realism. . . . Theater should not spend time photographing real life."[25]

In 1930 Meyerhold was still trying to counteract what he saw as the almost complete neglect of the art of movement and gesture by the naturalistic theater. He pointed out that humans move before they learn to speak and concluded that movement must have a natural primacy over speech in human development. By neglecting the art of stage movement, the actor and director deprive themselves of a basic means of human expression. In 1912 he declared that words were no more than "patterns on the canvas of movement." But in 1930 he denied his critics' charges that words were unimportant to him or that movement had priority over words in his work. Such ideas, he said, were only a part of his "pedagogic fictions" intended to combat the harmful influence of naturalistic theater. He led his students to believe that he thought movement more important than words in the hope that his protégés would then avoid performing like talking heads.[26] Ilya Ehrenburg wrote that Meyerhold eventually "ridiculed" his own concept of biomechanics.[27] Nevertheless, variations of biomechanics became a standard part of actor training in all Soviet drama schools.[28]

The highly fragmented structure of Meyerhold's productions was also a prime target for his enemies. It was so controversial that it could be attacked with the appearance of esthetic conviction even by those who knew or cared little about art but wanted to destroy the artist. Walter Benjamin reported the danger in 1927 when he wrote in the Berlin journal, *Die Literarische Welt*, about an "anti-Meyerhold front." The subject was again raised a year later in the same periodical by Brecht's friend and colleague, Bernhard Reich. Reich, who had emigrated to the Soviet Union, defended Meyerhold against those who attacked his episodic treatment of the Russian classic, Griboedov's *Woe to Wit*. The description of the play, offered by Reich, reads like a page torn from Brecht: "17 completely independent episodes out of the [original] four tightly-knit acts."[29] Each episode had its own particular stage business, symbolizing a certain aspect of society and social relations. In his review of the presentation of *Roar, China!* in Berlin in 1930, the noted critic Herbert Ihering remarked hostilely on the episodic form of that play and *The Inspector General* (1926), calling this style "almost a revue-theater."[30]

Such was the style—episodic, painterly, associative, aimed toward the creation of a thinking audience—which was finally stifled in January 1939, with Meyerhold's arrest and subsequent murder. The director-magician who could "serve up" his actors "in portions on small platform-plates" would offer such theatrical treats no more.

NOTES

1. Konstantin Rudnitsky, *Meyerhold the Director*, ed. Sydney Schultze (Ann Arbor, Mich.: Ardis, 1981), pp. 316–21.

2. Edward Braun, *The Theatre of Meyerhold: Revolution on the Modern Stage* (New York: Drama Book Specialists, 1979), p. 197.

3. Meyerhold changed the locale from a small town to a city, in order to make the events seem more universally relevant.

4. Quoted by Janko Lavrin, "Foreward" to N. Gogol, *The Government Inspector*, trans. J. D. Campbell (London: Wm. Heineman, 1953), p. 18.

5. Marjorie Hoover has suggested that the bagel in Khlestakov's lapel was symbolically parallel to the wooden spoon which Helene Weigel as Mother Courage wore on her jacket. In both cases, the objects symbolize their wearer's unquenchable appetites. See Hoover, *Meyerhold: The Art of Conscious Theater* (Amherst: University of Massachusetts

Press, 1974), p. 266. (Breughel's "Prodigal Son" also wears a wooden spoon on his jacket.)

   6. Rudnitsky, *Meyerhold the Director*, p. 391.

   7. *Stat'i, Pis'ma, Rechi, Besedy* 2 (1925): 110.

   8. Braun, *Meyerhold on Theatre*, p. 216.

   9. *SPRB* 2 (1927): 143.

   10. *SPRB* 2 (1925): 85, 88, 94. Meyerhold said that Zinaida Raikh coined the word pre-acting.

   11. Garin, *S Meierkhol'dom: Vospominaniia* (Moscow: Iskusstvo, 1974), p. 21.

   12. *SPRB* 2 (1931): 253–54.

   13. Aleksandr V. Fevral'skii, "S. M. Tret'iakov v teatre Meierkhol'da," in Sergei Tret'iakov, *Slyshish', Moskva?!*, ed. G. Mokrusheva (Moscow: Iskusstvo, 1966), pp. 200–202.

   14. Rudnitsky, *Meyerhold the Director*, pp. 462–67.

   15. All quotations from *The Bathhouse* are from *The Complete Plays of Vladimir Mayakovsky*, trans. Guy Daniels (New York: Washington Square Press, 1968), pp. 226, 228.

   16. *SPRB* 2 (1934): 56–57.

   17. *SPRB* 2 (1934): 297.

   18. *SPRB* 2 (1927): 158.

   19. *SPRB* 2 (1934): 297–98.

   20. Rudnitsky, *Meyerhold the Director*, p. 537.

   21. *SPRB* 2 (1936): 379.

   22. *SPRB* 2: 369.

   23. *SPRB* 2 (1925): 66–68.

   24. *SPRB* 2 (1925): 80.

   25. *SPRB* 2 (1933): 274–75.

   26. *SPRB* 2 (1930): 235–36.

   27. In *Meyerhold at Work*, ed. Paul Schmidt (Austin: University of Texas Press, 1980), p. 63. This book also has a good description of one of Meyerhold's training études, "Shooting the Bow," as his student Erast Garin remembers it (pp. 37–39).

   28. Braun, *The Theatre of Meyerhold*, p. 168.

   29. Bernhard Reich, "Meyerholds neue Inszenierung," *Die literarische Welt* 18 (1928).

   30. Herbert Ihering, *Von Reinhardt bis Brecht: Eine Auswahl der Theaterkritiken von 1909–1932* (Reinbek bei Hamburg: Rowohlt, 1967), p. 313.

4

"A DEMONSTRATIVELY PROLETARIAN SHABBINESS"

Brecht's first completed work as a director was also his first experience in radical adaptation of a classic text. He and his co-writer Lion Feuchtwanger were fortunate that the work they were altering—Marlowe's *Edward II*—was not famous or beloved, either in Germany or England. By choosing an obscure foreign play, they at least were spared the fury that swirled around Meyerhold each time he tampered with national properties. First of all, the two writers changed the title to *The Life of Edward II of England* because Brecht wanted to emphasize the epic aspect of the play.[1]

Though *The Life of Edward II* diverges from Marlowe's version in many ways, it generally follows the plot of the original, which in turn was loosely based on chronicle accounts, mainly Holinshed's. The Brecht-Feuchtwanger version begins in 1307 in London shortly after the death of Edward I. The new king recalls his lover Daniel Gaveston from exile in Ireland, thus arrogantly flouting the wishes of his late father, the peers of the realm, the princes of the Church, and his wife Queen Anna. Edward not only flaunts his affection for Gaveston (a mere butcher's son), he elevates him to positions of great power and prestige: Lord Chamberlain, Chancellor, Earl of Cornwall, peer of the Isle of Man, and Abbot of Coventry. Historically, as well as in Marlowe, Gaveston was a gentleman, a knight's son though not of the high nobility. By making the king's favorite a butcher's son, Brecht gave Gaveston's enemies an even stronger motivation for hating him and demanding his banishment. Edward's refusal to bow to the demands of his barons provokes a prolonged civil war which is led by the Earl Roger Mortimer, during which Gaveston is assassinated and Edward is captured. Shunted from prison to prison, Edward endures the most cruel and humiliating treatments. As in Marlowe's version, Edward's character becomes stronger as his humiliations increase. His will does not break even when his enemies place him in a foul sewer underneath the Tower of London. In the meantime, Edward's rejected wife has become Mortimer's mistress and accomplice. As the guardians of the young Prince Edward III, Anna and Mortimer rule the kingdom and eventually arrange the murder of Edward II. On receiving the news of his father's violent death, the young Edward rallies the nobles to his side, an action which results in Mortimer's execution.

The Brecht-Feuchtwanger version of *Edward II* is both a condensation and a broadening of the scope of the original. On the one hand, the two authors continued Marlowe's dramatic refinement of Holinshed's rambling account by further elimination or combination of characters and events. On the other hand, they restored the temporal sweep of the story. Holinshed recorded events in Edward's life which occurred over a twenty-three-year span (1307–1330). Marlowe rejected this long passage of time, so that all the events in his play occur within the space of about a year. The Brecht-Feuchtwanger version encompasses nineteen years (1307–1326) and is divided in a series of episodes which are captioned with information as to the year, month, day of the week, and place in which the events occur. From time to time the characters will remind each other of the vital statistics: "It is Thursday, it is London," Queen Anna says to the bewildered Edward.

Although the tendency in the Brecht-Feuchtwanger adaptation was to abbreviate Marlowe's text, some scenes were added, such as the one in which Gaveston makes out his will, or others which were so short that they amounted to hardly more than "lyrical punctuations." "One sees in the half darkness nothing but a troop of soldiers with their gleaming weapons marching past. One hears without quite being able to understand, the words of a strange wild song, and then the scene is over."[2]

Brecht recalled that when he wrote *The Life of Edward II*, he first had to deal with Marlowe's iambic verse lines. He thought the uneven, rough, and difficult verse of the old Schlegel-Tieck translations of Shakespeare were much more powerful than Rothe's smoothly flowing translation. So he decided to write the dialogue for *The Life of Edward II* in a halting sort of verse, to reflect the characters' contradictory feelings.[3] Although at the time of writing Brecht was not yet a Marxist, he was (he later recalled) aware of social inequities and wanted them reflected in the formal construction of his play. He claimed that the irregular meter signified two things: his rebellion against poetic conventions and his desire to reveal the violence and contrariness of human relationships.[4] Although Brecht gave himself credit for the rough verse, there is strong evidence that the idea for the irregular meter was Feuchtwanger's and that Feuchtwanger patiently taught Brecht the technique.[5]

For the production, Brecht rejected any elaborate royal trappings of jewels and furs and diadems, but he did not want a completely abstract setting either. The result was a simple set "such as the poor *Schaubudentheater* [fairground booth theaters] offer when they present a *Moritat* [a ballad about a gruesome crime]."[6] The Neher settings, like the costumes, were monotonal with a "shallow, frame-like inner proscenium . . . which held together the diverse images."[7] Such settings, and the plain sackcloth costumes, recall some of Meyerhold's Symbolist stagings. In one episode, a narrow footbridge high above the stage anticipated the rickety bridge which later played such an important part in *The Caucasian Chalk Circle*.

Thomas Mann saw *The Life of Edward II* at the *Kammerspiele*. For Mann, this spare, homely style expressed "a deliberate niggardliness, a demonstratively proletarian shabbiness . . . the last word in greasy makeshifts." Perhaps suspecting Soviet influence, Mann called the Brecht-Neher staging "a kind of dramatic Proletkult."[8] Edward's lover Gaveston, dressed in a coarse burlap coat, had his face painted like a harlequin to show that he was the king's plaything and fool. The peers of the realm sported "yellowish and greenish faces," colors which symbolized a fundamental rottenness.[9]

The Life of Edward II showed other parallels with avant-garde Soviet theater, particularly in its use of episode titles and gesture. The titles, which preceded each episode, gave precise information about dates and locales, about what had happened since previous episodes, and what would happen in the forthcoming episode: "9 May 1311: Since King Edward refuses to sign his name to the banishment of his favorite Gaveston, a thirteen-year war breaks out. Westminster."[10] The titles were announced by an actor who shouted them out "like a newspaper vendor" and who was dressed "in a kind of dirty painter's frock."[11] Only in Brecht's later productions were the scene titles usually projected on a screen rather than announced.

Brecht's preoccupation with gesture, which became so important to his later work, was already evident in *The Life of Edward II*. He made the actors show the exact motions which accompany a hanging; Gaveston must "be hanged *skillfully*." In another episode, Edward's seemingly faithful retainer Baldock betrays his master to the enemy by offering Edward a white handkerchief. Brecht instructed the actor playing Baldock: "you must show the treacherous gesture, the traitor's gesture. The public should see how a traitor behaves. The public must see—TREASON!"[12]

To express their weariness and fear, the soldiers marched mechanically to the beat of drums, with perfectly expressionless faces covered with white makeup.[13] In this English army, with their dirt-encrusted steel helmets, lived not only the miseries of 1550 [sic]—all armies of the European World War were contained in it."[14]

The music in *The Life of Edward II* shows Brecht's first steps toward using music as an element which ironically comments on, rather than follows, the action.[15] In a very tense scene Edward refuses to sign Parliament's order to banish Gaveston; instead, he tears the decree to shreds (in Marlowe, the King accedes to pressure and signs; Brecht's Edward is a more stubborn creature). "Now is England torn apart," declares the Archbishop. Lancaster adds: "Now indeed shall much blood flow in

England." At this moment, the act of defiance committed and gory civil war predicted, Lord Mortimer sings a little song to a closed session of Parliament:

> The English girls wore black and cried
> When their lovers died at Bannockbride
> Aheave and aho!
> The English king ordered his drummer boys
> To drown out the Bannockbride widows' noise
> With Arom Rombelow. (p. 21)

This is the only song in the Brecht-Feuchtwanger version that resembles a song in Marlowe. The other songs do not have counterparts in the original. The Mortimer of *The Life of Edward II* is dignified, intellectual, scholarly, cynically calculating, and keenly aware of his exalted position and power. And yet, to a session of Parliament, he sings! The other songs in the play are not so strangely out of place: soldiers sing as they march, a Balladeer, in the hope of garnering a few pennies, sings the latest popular ridicule of Edward. Yet another song is a bitter lament that the common people must die as a result of the intrigues of the powerful.

> Eddie is rolling his Gavy, which keeps him occupied
> Pray for us, pray for us, pray for us
> So Johnny got his in the rushes of the swamp at Bannockbride
> Pray for us, pray for us, pray for us. (p. 9)

In the original staging, the "Pray for us" song was part of an impressive scene. Marieluise Fleisser, who saw the 1924 production, has described the tall pasteboard mockups of London houses with numerous tiny windows. Suddenly all the windows simultaneously flew open and in each one there appeared a head, each head repeating the same litany: "Pray for us, pray for us," a prayer, yet a menacing complaint against the King. After the last "ghastly" refrain, "the windows slam shut with a single sharp crash."[16]

The Life of Edward II showed the first glimmerings of Brecht's technique of using music as an element in the overall montage. With the crucial help of Kurt Weill, the device came to dazzling fruition in *The Threepenny Opera*. According to Brecht, the cleverest innovation in *The Threepenny Opera* was that the music, sharply separated from other elements, was produced by a small group of musicians placed onstage in full view of the audience.[17] In reality, *The Threepenny Opera*'s onstage jazz band, projection screen, abrupt and ironic use of music, and shifting spotlight had all been tested in such earlier Meyerhold productions as *Trust D. E.* and *The Forest*. Technically, *The Threepenny Opera* was, as Lunacharsky noted, an echo of devices which were already standard in Soviet professional and amateur theater.

In Brecht's 1949 staging of *Mother Courage* (music by Paul Dessau), songs were announced and separated from the rest of the show by lowering cutouts of musical instruments, a banner, and lighted lanterns from the rigging loft. The musicians were seated in a box next to the stage. In describing the devices used in *Mother Courage*, Brecht used the word montage, calling it a method which helps destroy illusion, and he referred to the musical sections as "insertions."[18]

Conversely, the songs in *The Caucasian Chalk Circle* (1954), though they interrupted the dialogue and were also used to introduce episodes, seemed an integral part of the action and were not used for ironic contrast. Angelika Hurwicz has described how, in the scene in which Grusche meets her sweetheart, the narrator sang while the actors accompanied his text with "the most precise pantomime." The Singer gives voice to the emotions being mimed by the actors, allowing song and gesture to flow smoothly together.[19] But it is important to remember that in other respects Brecht retained for *Mother Courage* many of the tried and true devices of the montage theater of the twenties: grotesque mask and costuming to denote the rich and powerful characters; a highly episodic structure, with many fast scene changes; actors who used exaggerated poses and gestures and showed off their talent by playing multiple roles.[20]

The Life of Edward II showed off another strange device which caught the attention of and offended Thomas Mann. It was a curtain strung on a wire, perhaps the first time that sort of substitute for the traditional curtain was used on a modern stage.[21] The device, which seemed to Mann like so much "dirty linen," must have pleased Brecht very much, since it became a staple

of many of his later productions. Brecht argued that the traditional heavy curtain chops up the play (a curious objection by
one who favored chopping up the play).[22] Brecht's argument in
favor of the half-curtain, that it allows the spectator to see, at
least in part, the scene-changes and other work going on behind
it, is dubious.[23] If it is good to be able to see over the top of a
half-curtain, how much more educational not to have anything
blocking the view. Brecht's argument that a lightweight curtain
can reveal a play's "unique spirit" is more convincing. For *Puntila*, the material looked like rough linen, in *Der Hofmeister*, like
silk, in *Mother Courage*, like yellowed leather; in *The Fur Coat and
the Red Rooster*, a colorful caricature of a Prussian nobleman was
painted on the curtain.[24]

If Gogol had risen from his grave in 1926, he would have been
amazed to see what Meyerhold, at the height of his own artistic
power, had done with the text and performance style of *The
Inspector General*. Marlowe might have been even more flabber-
gasted by *The Life of Edward II of England*, if his spirit had visited
the Munich *Kammerspiele* in 1924. It was Brecht's apprenticeship
in the art of creative adaptation, and he must have been pleased
with the result because the challenges and problems of adaptation, especially of classic literature, formed an important part
of his dramatic theory, from the 1920s to the end of his life. In
The Messingkauf Dialogues, the Brecht persona called the *Dramaturg* talks admiringly about the wonderful artistic experimentation in Shakespearean theater. Experimentation in theater,
according to the *Dramaturg*, means altering plays, not once but
often, perhaps continually. This is not sacrilege but vitality.[25] In
short, he agreed with Meyerhold that playwrights generally write
for the dramatic techniques and technology of their own time,
thus challenging the creativity of all the directors who follow
them. For those who wanted to stage Molière's *Don Juan*, Brecht
advised a close reading of the text together with a study of
documents from Molière's time and of his relationship to his
time.[26] Brecht recommended this approach for actors as well as
directors because he thought the essential meaning of a dramatic
text could be determined by studying the text, its special features, and the period in which it was written.[27] Interestingly,
when Meyerhold first produced *Don Juan* in 1910, he applied to

the production (and urged on other directors of the play) almost exactly these procedures. He argued that *Don Juan* was one of those plays which could not be appreciated unless the spectator were given a feeling for the theatrical and historical atmosphere of seventeenth-century France and for Molière's relationship to his time. If not helped to such awareness, the playgoer will get bored. Meyerhold knew Molière's biography and the manner in which Molière's plays were staged and used this knowledge in directing *Don Juan*.[28]

In defending, in the 1950s, his own reworking of classic plays (in particular, Goethe's *Urfaust*), and perhaps to defend himself against charges of Formalism, Brecht accused other (unnamed) directors of souping up their productions of classic texts by using Formalist devices which have no intrinsic relation to the text. Though Brecht did not mention the arch-Formalist Meyerhold, he repeated Meyerhold's idea that the director-adaptor works with the text's essential socio-political idea and can use whatever artistic methods he wants to show the author's kernel ideas. There is nothing in the *Urfaust* essay with which Meyerhold would have quarreled, except Brecht's assertion that Formalist experiments were artistically destructive.[29]

Another device of the avant-garde for which Brecht eventually had to make excuses was the pictorial arrangement of actors. In an essay on his production of Przybyszewski's *Eternal Fairy Tale* Meyerhold had discussed at length the picture-like placement of actors onstage with a group of look-alike "nobles" arranged symmetrically on a staircase. In other scenes, the performers were carefully composed into contrasting groups according to their social and political relationships.[30] This sort of pictorialism typified Meyerhold's style from his earliest days as a director to the end of his career. When he was working on his productions at Komissarzhevskaia's theater (1906–1907), his custom was to bring to rehearsals prints by Botticelli, Memling, and other artists as a basis for the actors' gestures and groupings.[31] Although Brecht's theoretical writing and practice show his eagerness to transfer the painter's art of composition onto the stage, he repudiated the painterly arrangements of certain unnamed Formalist directors on the grounds that their pictorial effects were not really significant to the story.[32] Writing in 1953, Brecht asserted that stage groupings must somehow appear both natural and pictorial, which was a tactical non-shift from his earlier (1935–36) pronouncement that no attempt should be made to make groupings seem accidental as in life.[33] Despite official East German pressures against presenting Formalist stage pictures, the program for the 1954 Berliner Ensemble production of *The Caucasian Chalk Circle* showed that Breughel's "Crazy Grete" provided the model for Grusche.[34]

Brecht's postwar defense of his style was a continuation of wrangling begun in 1931 about the legitimacy of modernist art. Georg Lukács led the attack on modernism from the Soviet Union. He was a powerful critic whose political star in the 1930s was in the ascendant; hostile criticism from Lukács could mean prison or even death for an unlucky artist. The main part of this argument on modernism occurred during 1938 in *Das Wort* as a debate on Expressionism versus Realism. Brecht vehemently attacked Lukács in conversation with Benjamin and in his diary, but softened the blast in two draft articles for *Das Wort*, articles which were never published there. In fact, Brecht's part of the Expressionism-Realism debate was not published until twenty to thirty years later, well after his death.[35] The debate in *Das Wort* was preceded by Lukács' *International Literature* article, "Narrative or Descriptive Writing?" which was "aimed in particular at the [documentary] novels of Tretiakov,"[36] who had been arrested in 1937 and would be executed in 1939.

In his posthumously published replies to Lukács, Brecht suggested that the former was himself a kind of Formalist because he depended on formal criteria (derived from the work of a few nineteenth-century writers) for his definition of Realism. The truth, Brecht commented, can be expressed in a variety of styles.[37] He offered a criterion for judging whether or not a piece of art is realistic, a criterion which would allow for a great deal of creative freedom, would be acceptable from a Marxist standpoint, and might even permit many styles to be squeezed in under the label Socialist Realism. He suggested that in deciding what is or is not realistic in the theater, the means (the play's content and style of presentation) should be judged according to whether or not they fulfill certain socially desirable ends. Brecht implied that Lukács' critical judgments against modernism were elitist and bourgeois, and argued that one need not be afraid to bring an unfamiliar style before a proletarian audience. The intelligentsia may think they are the best judge of art for the workers, but workers do not need middlemen. Artists and workers can speak directly to one another.[38]

Brecht has left a fairly detailed description of what Meyerhold called the "epically cold" acting style. In Jessner's *Oedipus* when Helene Weigel as Jocasta's maid discovered her mistress's body and ran onstage to report the terrible sight, she called out the news emotionlessly. Only her white-painted face and physical gestures expressed her shock.[39]

It was this sort of emotional distancing from the role that Brecht sought from his performers. He advised that a player can avoid losing himself in the role if he constantly reminds himself that he is only showing, quoting, and repeating dialogue and events to the audience. In this way the performer will not get hypnotized and neither will the audience. The Philosopher of the *Messingkauf Dialogues* did not object to the actor empathizing with a character as part of his preparation for a role, so long as the empathy was finally dispensed with, or at least kept to a minimum. Of all the sources of emotion, empathy is the least necessary, according to the Philosopher.[40]

Like Meyerhold, Brecht was reacting against Stanislavsky's method of training actors, a system which aims at eliminating psychological distance between performer and role. Though Brecht scoffed at Stanislavsky's exercises (such as pretending that a hat has turned into a rat), the drills he suggested for actors were probably not far from the sort of thing Stanislavsky's students did: pretending to do laundry or enacting scenes from the Bible. But Brecht did encourage performers to rehearse lines in their native dialects or in the third person. He also recommended athletic training for performers because actors need a fine control over their bodies. But his suggestions in this regard are general, and he never attempted to develop, as Meyerhold did, a complex system of physical exercises. Rather, he warned against overemphasizing physical culture in training actors,[41] and his passing reference to Russian-style actors' exercises, designed to create an illusion of spontaneity, is lightly mocking.[42]

Nevertheless, Brecht's mature genius as a playwright collided with his distancing theories. From the late 1930s, he began to create those gigantic characters—Puntila, Galileo, Mother Courage, Shen Te, Azdak—who cannot help but stir the emotions of an audience. For the production of *Herr Puntila and His Servant Matti* (1948) Brecht recommended that the actor who plays Puntila be careful in the drunk scenes not to be so full of life and charming that the audience is completely swept away and so loses its critical ability.[43]

In order to reconcile theory and practice, Brecht toward the end of his life objected to the idea that epic acting and empathy are mutually exclusive. He urged a dialectic approach in which Demonstrating and Experiencing are viewed as opposite poles, which unite in the actor's performance.[44] Even so, it was Meyerhold's "epically cold" style which Brecht (at least in theory) always promoted. He suggested that actors rehearse by prefacing lines with the appropriate stage directions, in the third person and in the past tense,[45] speak verse lines in prose or native dialect,[46] or simply watch as someone else performs the role. At the beginning of rehearsals the actor's empathy is important and should be supported by props and costumes. But later on, the empathy must disappear while the actor moves from an intuitive toward a conscious and critical presentation.[47]

This lack of emotionalism is built into the dialogue of Brecht's plays. At times of greatest emotional stress the characters may speak to each other with quaint formality, as in the reunion scene in *The Caucasian Chalk Circle* (1948) when Grusche and her sweetheart address each other politely from opposite sides of a brook, or with terrible understatement as when Mother Courage remarks after the execution of her son, "I guess I haggled too long."

In the only book-length work on Brecht which conscientiously deals with the Russian influences, John Fuegi writes that Brecht "seems, in his theater practice from about 1939 on, to retreat from those theatrical devices that his early theory had set such store by."[48] Judging, however, by the text of the plays themselves, photos of the productions, and accounts of Brecht's rehearsal methods, I do not see that there was a significant divergence from his earlier theories of epic theater. The degree of stylization in the writing and staging of *Mother Courage* and

The Caucasian Chalk Circle (though rather tame compared to his prewar style) is amazing, considering the extremely conservative cultural atmosphere in which they were staged. After all, Brecht wanted to have his work produced. The change, after 1939, lay in Brecht's new power to create larger-than-life characters who engage the audience's sympathy despite the episodic structure, grotesquerie, unemotional dialogue, abstract setting—in short, the whole stylized framework in which these characters are presented.

Given their preference for understated acting and their dislike of empathizing, it is not surprising that both Meyerhold and Brecht found their ideal in the virtuoso art of the Chinese actor Mei Lan-fang. Apparently when Brecht was in Moscow in 1935, he saw at least two performances by Mei, "probably in the company of the men who had invited Mei Lan-fang to Moscow (Tretiakov, Eisenstein, and possibly Meyerhold himself)."[49] At the matinee, Mei appeared dressed in casual Western clothes and enacted some of the female characters in his repertoire. Brecht noted two clearly observable figures: the demonstrated (female character) and the demonstrator (Mei). In the evening, Mei gave a similar performance, but this time he was dressed in female costume and makeup. The actor had almost (but not quite) disappeared. Brecht felt that the actors (Mei and his ensemble) had perfected the art of "double showing," though to be exact there were really three figures present: the actor as ordinary person, the character being performed, and the actor as performer, showing off his skills.[50] It was this Moscow performance of the Chinese ensemble which inspired Brecht's first writing on the Alienation Effect (V-Effect).[51]

Brecht offered examples of how the V-Effect operates in life: a stepfather comes into your life and you suddenly see your mother as a man's wife, or the sheriff arrests one of your teachers. When such things happen, events and people we have taken for granted become suddenly strange, but this transformation into strangeness ultimately results in deepened understanding. The purpose of art is to force the spectator to a shock of recognition through the use of estranging devices.[52]

In a further echo of Russian Formalist theories, Brecht described how, in the old realistic theater, the V-Effect showed up as "flaws," whenever the audience became aware of the devices being used. In what Brecht chose to call "Aristotelian" theater, this unintentional revelation of the device was greatly resented as a failure, not because tricks should not be used but because the tricks did not work. Brecht claimed that his own style purposely revealed theatrical devices.[53]

Brecht may not have used the word *Verfremdung* until the late thirties, but he was drawn to the idea from a much earlier time. Notes written in 1920 anticipate Meyerhold's 1921 writings, inspired by Marinetti. Brecht's notes of 1920 suggest techniques for cooling off emotional scenes on the stage, including tragic scenes. He claimed that if he were in charge of a theater, he would engage two clowns, who would appear during intermission and mock the play, its heroes, and its performance style.[54] Following his theory that "today it is more important for the settings to tell the spectator that he is in a theater, than that he is in Aulis," Brecht suggested (around 1929) that the best idea is to reveal the stage machinery (a revelation which had wowed St. Petersburg audiences when they saw Meyerhold's production of Blok's *The Fairground Booth* in 1906).

Tretiakov's 1923 essay "Vsevolod Meierkhol'd," attributes to Meyerhold certain important changes in theater art, among them the transformation of the audience from a "chance gathering" into a "firmly established collective, which interacts with the play." Perhaps it is not a coincidence that in 1931, shortly after he met Tretiakov, Brecht envisioned for his "dialectic" or "new" drama[55] a productive audience-"collective" which interacts with the show. It would be a purposeful community of theater experts, rather than the usual random gathering of spectators who happen to find themselves in the same theater, waiting to be entertained.[56]

The new theater Brecht hoped might encourage a better society had certain characteristic esthetic underpinnings which (with variations) remained stable throughout his life as director and playwright. The most important devices of this new theater were related to the idea of montage, of a strict separation of artistic elements, and also to the concept of art as an open-ended means of communicating with an intellectually alert, rational, and responsive spectator.

Montage made possible the hallmarks of a Brechtian production: the episodic structure; the peculiar contrast of realism and abstraction; masks; hyperbole; the ironic use of music. Brecht leaned at least as heavily on the technique of fragmentation as did Meyerhold, and wrote extensively on its purposes and effects. He specified that a play should not only be episodic, but the episodes must be linked in such a way that the audience can plainly see the "knots." This was supposed to prevent spectators from being mindlessly drawn into the action, so that they could be intellectually free to impose their own judgments.[57] Brecht approvingly quoted Alfred Döblin's test for epic-ness: an epic work (in contrast to a dramatic one) can be cut up into individual pieces and each little piece will remain alive.[58]

A Man's a Man (1926) has eleven titled scenes and a variety of locales; each episode is a small story. In the 1931 production of the same play the theater manager walked onstage with the script and read the scene titles.[59] In *Arturo Ui* (written in the 1940s) episodes follow one another in rapid succession; each scene takes place in a different locale and the character groupings constantly change. Much the same observation could be made of most of Brecht's plays. In *The Caucasian Chalk Circle* this episodic treatment is done in an especially clever way: the first part almost seems unrelated to the episode-pictures which follow, and yet in many subtle ways it is enmeshed with them. Though the various episodes in *The Caucasian Chalk Circle* are related thematically, theoretically they are performable on their own.

The construction of Brecht's *Schweyk in the Second World War* (written in the early 1940s) is fragmented not only by division into episodes but by the further division of the play into "regions" (higher, middle, lower, and lowest). The higher region is the orbit of Hitler and his henchmen, the middle region is Prague, the lower region is the Nazi prison and interrogation room, and the lowest region of all is where Schweyk and Hitler finally meet: the road to Stalingrad.

Movement (groupings of actors, mime, gesture, and choreography) and the training of actors in the art of movement are also hallmarks of Brechtian theater. Brecht's famous theory of Gestus, which goes far beyond mere physical gesture, could never succeed in practice if the actors and director (and perhaps, as Meyerhold suggests, the dramatist also) were not sensitive to the art of movement in its widest Meyerholdian sense: a union of words with physical movement, lines, color, groupings of actors and objects—the whole non-verbal pattern which serves as the canvas upon which the words are written and which helps to express what words alone cannot signify. In the *Messingkauf Dialogues* the *Dramaturg* criticizes, as Meyerhold had done many years before, the naturalistic theater's tendency to neglect the art of gesture and movement while depending solely on the actor's voice and facial expressions.[60]

Not all actors in a Brecht production were human, however; objects also had to be performers and expressive ones at that. In Brecht's presentation of his play *The Mother* (1932) there was only very sparing use of props, limited to those things which had a definite utilitarian purpose. Objects were actors or they were not used at all. Brecht's description of the settings of *The Mother* brings to mind Meyerhold's Constructivist sets: a few tall iron pipes, immovable, placed vertically at irregularly spaced intervals along the stage, together with horizontal, movable pipes which could be fastened together with canvas. This made possible quick scene changes. Freestanding doors were hung between the vertical pipes. One of the few things that Brecht liked about the New York Theater Union production of *The Mother* (1935) was Mordecai Gorelik's settings, which were similar to Neher's.[61] Though he had not previously known of Brecht, Gorelik knew and admired Meyerhold's work and perhaps for that reason was more attuned to Brecht's style than were others associated with the Theater Union.[62]

Screens or panels were used consistently as the basis for abstract backgrounds in the work of both men. These screens were used to frame the stage-picture, for film projections, for quick scene and episode changes. Their geometric shapes contrasted with the realistic objects placed in front of them. That this mixture of abstraction and realism was for Brecht an important element in the staging of *The Mother* is shown by his correspondence with the Theater Union, urging the right "mixture of realism and stylization."[63] For Meyerhold, such panels served to block out the backstage area, thus bringing the actors and the action to the forestage and closer to the audience, and the use of screens or panels changed with changes in his style between the early 1920s and the end of his career. Until 1924 he customarily combined movable panels with an otherwise bare stage; the audience could see the unadorned brick back wall of the stage along with all the theatrical apparatus: the stage "kitchen." The Soviet critic Boris Alpers, writing in 1931, reported that audiences in the Meyerhold Theater could no longer see the sort of bare stage productions which caused so much discussion in the twenties; nothing was left of the bare stage with its unpainted brick wall. The wall had been whitewashed and was generally hidden by screens, hangings, and other constructions. In contrast to the staging of *Trust D. E.*, in which movable walls were used for a "breathtaking dynamism of motion,"[64] *The Inspector General* inaugurated a new era in Meyerhold's work, away from movable settings, acrobatic actors, and large gestures appropriate to a big stage area, toward the opposite: an immobility, a highly circumscribed stage with fairly heavy, immovable screens blocking off the backstage and sidestage areas. The once acrobatic actors turned into poseurs, and each episode became a small tableau. Stylistically, it was in many ways a turning back to the narrower stage and "static theater" of his early Symbolist days.

The technique of using panels as multipurpose background settings, which narrowed the stage space, was already in use in Germany when Brecht began his career as a director in Munich. When Otto Falckenberg staged Brecht's *Drums in the Night* at the *Kammerspiele* in Munich in 1922, he used two-meter-high pasteboard screens to represent the walls of a room. Behind these screens was a stylized cityscape.[65] The panels, which made the small acting area of the *Kammerspiele* stage even smaller, and the Cubist cityscape behind them contrasted with the few drab pieces of real furniture on the forestage. All in all, Falckenberg's production followed an Expressionist style which had strong echoes of Russian Symbolist and Cubist stage design. Though Brecht did not have a hand in this production, he was present at rehearsals.[66]

In choosing materials for stage settings in *The Roundheads and the Peakheads* (1936), Brecht used background screens made of parchment; these screens were intended to be reminiscent of old books, thus lending the parable some of the prestige of ancient stories. When Brecht saw the *King Lear* production of the Moscow Yiddish Theater in 1935, he admired its use of a folding wooden tabernacle-like construction which evoked images of medieval Judaism.[67] Caspar Neher's style of stage design, with its combination of careful realism in the smaller properties and stylization in the larger setting, harmonized well with (perhaps helped develop) Brecht's liking for evocative stage design.

The setting for the Berlin production of *Mother Courage* (directed by Brecht in 1949) was based on a design created by Teo Otto in 1941 for a production of that play in Zurich. There was a stage "frame" made of large fixed panels covered with natural materials: tent canvas, wood, rope, and so on. Buildings such as the vicarage and farmer's cottage also used natural materials and were realistically constructed, but only so much of the building was indicated or suggested as was useful for the action of the play.[68]

The settings for the first production of *Herr Puntila and His Servant Matti* (Zurich, 1948), directed by K. Hirschfeld, reflected Brecht's favorite mixture of abstraction and realism; again, the stylized background was constructed of panels, this time of birchbark, with sun, moon, and cloud constructions suspended in front of them (as Brecht approvingly noted). The props and costumes, in contrast, were realistic. An automobile which appeared onstage had only its front end constructed, but that section was built with real materials.[69]

Galileo, one of Brecht's greatest plays and one which is often singled out as marking the playwright's embrace of theatrical conservatism, in its structure and staging did not significantly depart from the style of modernist theater that Brecht had favored since the 1920s. For its 1947 Los Angeles production, directed by Joseph Losey under Brecht's close supervision, the author called for a non-representational background setting which would remind the audience that it was in a theater.[70] In contrast, he wanted (as usual) the furniture and other properties (including doors) to be realistic and charming. The costumes were to be individualized and look as though they had been worn, but there is no indication that these realistic-looking props and costumes were supposed to be period pieces.[71]

By 1954 what Boris Alpers had once praised as "social mask

theater'' was flourishing at the Berliner Ensemble. The setting for *The Caucasian Chalk Circle* was highly stylized, but was supplemented with many realistic details.[72] The audience could see that some essential pieces of a rope bridge really were missing as was one of the ropes holding the bridge together. But this authentic-looking prop was attached to a most unrealistic small mock-up of two cliffs, which stood in front of a cloth backdrop. Mountain scenery was painted on the backdrop in the highly conventionalized manner of Japanese painting, and the painted mountains fluttered like banners.

Thus Brecht's production of *The Caucasian Chalk Circle* remained "social mask" theater to the core. The characters were what they wore, as surely as in *A Man's a Man*, where the white-painted soldiers' faces expressed their fear, the sergeant's partially masked face, his fearsome authority, Galy Gay's physical transformations, his change from a person into a nameless, faceless fighting machine. In *The Caucasian Chalk Circle* the powerful citizens of Grusinia were monsters whose weird masks and luxurious clothing contrasted with the plain-looking peasants and servants. Brecht directed that the degree to which the lower-class characters of *The Caucasian Chalk Circle* are made grotesque depends on the degree to which they have been corrupted by contact with their morally deformed masters.

Brecht's theory and practice of stage lighting techniques also paralleled Meyerhold's closely. Just as, in 1910, the Russian director wrote that he favored even white light and clearly visible light sources in the theater because such lighting promotes psychological interaction between actor and spectator, so Brecht in 1940 wrote that he favored that kind of lighting, and for the same reasons: bright light from obvious sources promotes the V-Effect and prevents illusion.[73] The acting area for *Puntila* was always completely lit with an even white light.[74] The same sort of lighting was planned for Strittmatter's *Katzgraben* (1953), but could not be achieved with the equipment available at the *Deutsches Theater*.[75]

Indeed, the main creative principle of the European avant-garde theater of the 1920s and 1930s was a principle of light, of clarity. Nothing was to be left in darkness, nothing was to be kept hidden—not the performers, not the audience, not the time-honored devices of theater—not even the mechanical sources of the light itself. Let there be in the theater light, joy, and spaciousness, Meyerhold had commanded, and Brecht, too, pushed for that sense of intellectual discovery which can occur only when a performance is bathed in light.

It is fitting that Brecht returned the white light of creativity to Soviet art. When, in the mid-1950s, Brecht's plays and poetry reappeared in the Soviet Union after a publishing blackout of some twenty years, the effect on Soviet literature was, according to Efim Etkind, "gigantic." Thus, even before the Berliner Ensemble made its first tour, in the fall of 1957, to Moscow and Leningrad, the liberating effect of this poet who was, miraculously, both avant-garde and "classic" (that is, officially accepted) was already being felt in the world of Soviet art.

As far as Russian theater was concerned, the advent of Brecht's ensemble and dramatic theory meant that Soviet theater people could begin to shake off the smothering grip of the Moscow Art Theater, whose slice-of-life realism had been, since the 1940s, the only permitted style. Under the sheltering wings of the classic Brecht, Soviet theater workers gathered up and continued to weave the luminous threads of Meyerholdian drama.[76]

NOTES

1. Bernhard Reich, *Im Wettlauf mit der Zeit* (Berlin: Henschelverlag, 1970), p. 250.

2. Hans Werner Grüninger, "Brecht und Marlowe," *Comparative Literature* 21 (Summer 1969): 232–44. Grüninger is quoting Julius Bab.

3. Brecht, "Über reimlose Lyrik mit unregelmässigen Rhythmen," *Versuche*, vol. 12 (Frankfurt a.M.: Suhrkamp, 1958), pp. 143–44.

4. *Versuche*, 12: 144.

5. For a discussion of Feuchtwanger's part in the adaptation of *The Life of Edward II of England*, see Faith G. Norris, "The Collaboration of Lion Feuchtwanger and Bertolt Brecht," in *Lion Feuchtwanger: Critical Essays* (Los Angeles: Hennessey and Ingalls, 1972), pp. 277–305, and John Fuegi, "Feuchtwanger, Brecht and the 'Epic' Media the Novel and Film," ibid., p. 308.

6. Reich, *Wettlauf*, p. 239.

7. Carl Niessen, *Brecht auf der Bühne* (Cologne: Institut für Theaterwissenschaft an der Universität Köln, 1959), p. 13.

8. Thomas Mann, "German Letter," *The Dial* 77 (November 1924): 418–19. The Proletkult Theater passed "from Eisenstein's eccentricities in the spirit of Meyerhold to revolutionary local-color dramas. . . . The Meyerhold Theater for a long time led the . . . Proletkult Theater. . . . Sergei Eisenstein, Meyerhold's student, whose development occurred within the theatrical system of his teacher, directed the Proletkult Theater from 1922–1924." Boris Alpers, *Teatr sotsial'noi maski* (Moscow: Gos. izd. khud. lit., 1931), p. 97.

9. Reich, *Wettlauf*, p. 255; Mann, "German Letter," p. 419.

10. Bertolt Brecht, *Edward II: A Chronicle Play*, trans. Eric Bentley (New York: Grove Press, 1966), pp. 16–17. All citations from *The Life of Edward II of England* are from this edition.

11. Rudolf Frank, *Spielzeit meines Lebens* (Heidelberg: Lambert Schneider, 1960), p. 313.

12. Reich, *Wettlauf*, p. 257.

13. Anna Lacis, *Revolutionär im Beruf*, ed. Hildegard Brenner (Munich: Rogner und Bernhard, 1971), p. 37.

14. Frank, *Spielzeit*, p. 270.

15. Klaus Völker believes that in *The Life of Edward II*, Brecht "still used music in the traditional way," that it served only to "add lightness, variety, and poetry." This is generally true; still, there are clear signs of a movement toward music as separate, ironic commentary. See Klaus Völker, *Brecht: A Biography*, trans. John Howell (New York: Continuum, 1978), p. 125.

16. Marieluise Fleisser, "Aus der Augustenstrasse," in Reinhold Grimm, ed., *Bertolt Brecht: Leben Edwards des Zweiten von England; Vorlage, Texte und Materialien* (Frankfurt a.M.: Suhrkamp, 1968), p. 264.

17. *Schriften zum Teatr* 2 (1931): 102.

18. *SzT* 6 (c. 1949): 51–52.

19. Angelika Hurwicz, *Brecht inszeniert* (Velber bei Hannover: Friedrich, 1964), no pagination.

20. John Fuegi, *The Essential Brecht* (Los Angeles: Hennessey and Ingalls, 1912), pp. 144–47.

21. Wolfgang Petzet, *Theater: Die Münchner Kammerspiele, 1911–1972* (Munich: Verlag Kurt Desch, 1973) p. 153.

22. For a thorough treatment of the contradictions between Brecht's theory and practice, see John Fuegi's "The Caucasian Chalk Circle in Performance," *Brecht Heute. Brecht Today*, ed. Reinhold Grimm et al. (Frankfurt a.M.: Athenäum, 1971), pp. 137–49, as well as Fuegi's *The Essential Brecht* and Martin Esslin's review of *The Essential Brecht* in

Brecht-Jahrbuch 1974, ed. Reinhold Grimm et al. (Frankfurt a.M.: Suhr-kamp, 1974), pp. 154–57.

23. *SzT* 6: 220–21.

24. *SzT* 6: 221.

25. Bertolt Brecht, *The Messingkauf Dialogues*, ed. and trans. John Willett (London: Methuen, 1965), pp. 37–38, 60. The *Messingkauf Dialogues* were written c. 1937. See also *SzT* 1 (1927): 95, *SzT* 6 (1948):46.

26. *SzT* 6 (c. 1953): 342.

27. *SzT* 6: 216.

28. *Stat'i, Pis'ma, Rechi, Besedy* 1 (1910): 192.

29. *SzT* 6 (1954); 321–23. Brecht's defense of his style is a sad replay of Meyerhold's 1936 attempt to defend his work against charges of "Meyerholdism" (i.e., Formalism). Meyerhold's self-defense did not always do him honor either, since he accused other directors (including his former students Radlov and Okhlopkov) of being the real Meyer-holdists, borrowing his tricks but not his genius (but, at the same time, he bravely defended Shostakovich, whose work had just been banned). Okhlopkov and Radlov retaliated with their own attacks on Meyerhold. See Konstantin Rudnitsky, *Meyerhold the Director*, ed. Sydney Schultze (Ann Arbor, Mich.: Ardis, 1981), pp. 537–38, and Edward Braun, *The Theatre of Meyerhold* (New York: Drama Book Specialists, 1979), pp. 261–62.

30. *SPRB* 1 [1912]: 246–48.

31. Marjorie L. Hoover, "V. E. Meyerhold: A Russian Predecessor of Avant-Garde Theater," *Comparative Literature* 17 (Summer 1965): 246.

32. *SzT* 6: 216–17; *SzT* 6 (1948): 19; *SzT* 6 (c. 1950): 80.

33. *SzT* 7 (1953): 94, 97.

34. More detailed observations on the importance of pictorial effects can be found in Brecht's notes for *The Mother*, *Puntila*, and *The Resistible Rise of Arturo Ui*. After the Berliner Ensemble production of *The Mother* (1951), Brecht admitted he had striven for a pictorial effect, but argued that this pictorialness did not disturb the essential realism of the play. In his notes on *Puntila* Brecht remarked that every view of the stage must capture, in its spatial composition and color, a visually worthwhile picture. Similarly, he wanted the scenes of *Arturo Ui* to look like his-torical paintings. *SzT* 6: 297; *SzT* 6 (1948): 238; *SzT* 4: 168.

35. On the main points of the debate and Brecht's very prudent role in it, see Ronald Hayman, *Brecht: A Biography* (New York: Oxford Uni-versity Press, 1983), pp. 211–12, and (for an exhaustively detailed dis-cussion) David Pike, *German Writers in Soviet Exile, 1933–1945* (Chapel Hill: University of North Carolina Press, 1982), pp. 259–306.

36. Völker, *Brecht: A Biography*, pp. 248–49.

37. *SzT* 4 (1938): 149–61, first pubished 1958.

38. *SzT* 4 (1938): 158–59.

39. *SzT* 1 (1929): 214–15. With regard to Weigel's whiteface makeup for *Oedipus*, Hayman observes, "it is improbable that Brecht had never told her about the clown-white faces of the soldiers in *Edward II*; it is equally improbable that Brecht and Weigel had never discussed how she should make up for *Oedipus*." Hayman suggests that the white-faced soldiers of *Edward II*, "one of Brecht's first alienation effects, . . . probably . . . derives from Meyerhold." *Brecht*, pp. 101, 139.

40. *The Messingkauf Dialogues*, pp. 55–57; *SzT* 3 (1936): 54–55.

41. *SzT* 4: 52.

42. *The Messingkauf Dialogues*, pp. 28–29.

43. *SzT* 6 (1948): 239.

44. *SzT* 7 (1952–54): 60.

45. *SzT* 3 (1940): 160–61.

46. *SzT* 3 (n.d.): 168.

47. Ruth Berlau et al., *Theaterarbeit: 6 Aufführungen des Berliner Ensembles*, 2d rev. and enlarged ed. (Berlin: Henschelverlag Kunst und Gesellschaft, 1961), p. 244.

48. Fuegi, *The Essential Brecht*, p. 128.

49. Ibid., p. 126.

50. *SzT* 4: 56–57.

51. *SzT* 5: 166–82; note, p. 310. For a succinct history of Brecht's theories of *Entfremdung* and *Verfremdung*, see John Willett, "Brecht, Alienation, and Karl Marx," in *Brecht in Context: Comparative Approaches* (London and New York: Methuen, 1984), pp. 218–21. Though Mei demonstrated classic Chinese theater abroad, back home in China, people wanted him to perform in Western realistic theater, according to a report by a Russian engineer and former student of architecture and interior design, Peter Rodyenko. Rodyenko was stationed in Shanghai as a military advisor, where he became well known for his skill as an interior designer. Some high Chinese officials, having invested heavily and unprofitably in traditional shows at a local theater, approached Rodyenko and asked him to direct a Western-style play called *Napoleon's Rise and Fall* with Mei Lan-Fang as the leading actor. Rodyenko's description of the noisy, exuberant crowd that came to see *Napoleon's Rise and Fall* would have delighted Brecht, who idealized the sporting-crowd audience. The fantastic anachronisms the Chinese stage crew mixed in with Rodyenko's carefully designed "authentic" settings and costumes would have delighted Brecht even more: Napoleon's soldiers, dressed in period uniforms, march onstage mounted on Mongolian ponies; Napoleon himself enters, riding in a brand new automobile which sports

a sign proclaiming "Sime Honigsberg, sole distributor of the famous American Studebaker car in the Far East, has placed this noble vehicle, the latest imported model, at the disposal of Mr. Mei Lan-Fang, free of charge." Napoleon is finally forced to surrender when, "suspended by wires and flying a huge British flag—a large aeroplane is pulled across the stage and begins to drop bombs upon the Old Guard." Rodyenko's anger was gently turned back by Chinese friends who reminded him of the triviality of a hundred-year anachronism "compared with eternity and the history of China." "Napoleon in Shanghai: A Russian Designer's Waterloo," *Theatre Arts Monthly* 17 (April 1938): 298–306.

52. *SzT* 3 (1940): 174–76.

53. *SzT* 3: 183–85. Compare this passage and similar statements in *The Messingkauf Dialogues*, p. 76, with Boris Tomashevsky's essay on the revelation of devices in "The Vitality of Plot Devices" (part of his 1925 essay on "Thematics") in *Russian Formalist Criticism*, pp. 92–95.

> Two literary styles may be distinguished in terms of the perceptibility of the devices. The first, characteristic of writers of the nineteenth century, is distinguished by its attempt to conceal the device. . . . But this is only one style. . . . It is opposed to another style, an unrealistic style, which does not bother about concealing the devices and which frequently tries to make them obvious. . . . In such a case, the author has called attention to the device or . . . —the technique is "laid bare."
>
> In the early stages of Futurism . . . and in contemporary literature, the laying bare of techniques had become traditional.

54. *SzT* 2 (1920): 18–19.

55. "Dialectic" and "new" drama were terms Brecht began to use after meeting Tretiakov. The words are fairly synonymous with the earlier "epic theater."

56. *SzT* 1 (1931): 258–59.

57. *SzT* 7 (1948): 50.

58. *SzT* 3 (1936): 53. Peter Szondi notes that, in Strindberg's *A Dream Play*, individual scenes have no causal relationship to each other; rather they are "isolated stones, lined up along the thread of the progressing ego." The unity in such a play, as in dreams or picaresque novels, is not in the plot but in the ego. Brecht's and Meyerhold's plays, while episodic, still keep what Szondi calls "the dialectic of interaction between people." See *Theorie des modernen Dramas* (Frankfurt a.M.: Suhrkamp, 1956), pp. 47, 51.

59. *SzT* 4 (n.d.): 80.

60. *The Messingkauf Dialogues*, p. 28.

61. *SzT* 2 (1935-36): 147.

62. Lee Baxandall, "Brecht in America, 1935," *The Drama Review* 12 (Fall 1967): 78.

63. James K. Lyon, "Der Briefwechsel zwischen Bertolt Brecht und der New Yorker Theater Union von 1935," *Brecht-Jahrbuch*, 1975, ed. John Fuegi et al. (Frankfurt a.M.: Suhrkamp, 1975), p. 140.

64. Rosemarie Tietze, ed., *Vsevolod Meyerhold: Theaterarbeit 1917–1930* (Munich: Carl Hanser, 1974), p. 16.

65. *SzT* 2 [1922]: 65.

66. There are conflicting reports about the degree of Brecht's influence on the first production of *Drums in the Night*. According to Erwin Faber, who played Kragler, Brecht had no influence on the staging of the play and did not try to interfere with Falckenberg's direction. W. Stuart McDowell, "Actors on Brecht: The Munich Years," *The Drama Review* 20 (September 1976): 104. Feuchtwanger's wife was also present at rehearsals, and she reported that Brecht was very disruptive. "Pretty soon Brecht had almost taken over the entire production and the director—a mature man—was practically his assistant." Carl Weber, "Brecht as Director," *The Drama Review* 12 (Fall 1967): 106.

67. *SzT* 3 (n.d.): 229–39.

68. *SzT* 6 [1949]: 53.

69. *SzT* 6 (1948): 238.

70. *SzT* 4 (1956): 235.

71. In *The Essential Brecht*, John Fuegi argues (as do several other scholars) that Brecht's great plays of the 1940s and 1950s represent a return to the principles of traditional theater, empathy, tight structure, and neatly blended artistic elements, and that the great plays "must be abominably produced indeed in order to elicit a cool response." Here Fuegi is speaking specifically of *The Good Person of Sezuan* (p. 134). As I have said, I am not convinced that Brecht's greatest plays represent an important departure from his "radical" dramatic theories of the 1920s and 1930s (theories which were never all that radical, anyway). The very fact that (as Fuegi points out) Brecht fretted about *Galileo* not being epic enough indicates that he remained very concerned with upholding his accustomed ideas on theater. The strong emotional impact and charm that *Galileo* (and *Mother Courage* and *Puntila*) had for audiences when the Berliner Ensemble performed could owe at least as much to the high talents of the performers as to any inherently emotional quality of the text. Perhaps a less perfect production (not necessarily an abominable one) does not so much destroy the emotionality of these plays as let the essential coolness shine through.

72. Hurwicz, no pagination given: see also Ruth Berlau, Bertolt Brecht, et al., *Theaterarbeit: 6 Aufführungen des Berliner Ensembles*, 2d rev. and

enlarged ed. (Berlin: Henschelverlag Kunst and Gesellschaft, 1961), p. 163.

73. *SzT* 3 (1940): 165–66; see also *SzT* 3: 241.

74. *SzT* 6 (1948): 236.

75. *SzT* 7: 163.

76. Efim Etkind, "Brecht and the Soviet Theater," *Bertolt Brecht: Political Theory and Literary Practice*, ed. Betty Nance Weber and Hubert Heinen (Athens: University of Georgia Press, 1980), pp. 81, 84.

5

CONCLUSIONS: A TROJAN HORSE

The fame of the German poet-playwright-director-theoretician Bertolt Brecht now surpasses the reputation of his older contemporary, the Russian director and theoretician Vsevolod Meyerhold. Yet this was not always the case. From the early years of the twentieth century until about 1940, Meyerhold was the most famous living theater worker in the West. The two ideas that form the basis of Brecht's theoretical work—the idea that a dramatic performance should be a fully conscious creation of all concerned (playwright, actors, directors, spectators) and the idea of theater as a force for social betterment—are found in Meyerhold's letters written in the late 1890s. This is not to say that he was the "inventor" of such concepts. These things were "in the air," as Piscator put it, and of course have a long history. But Meyerhold in his time surpassed his contemporaries in his ability to combine certain esthetic and political ideas and transfer them successfully to the stage.

Diderot in his *Paradoxe sur le comédien* (1773/78) pointed out that the stage does not and should not reflect nature and, for very practical reasons, opposed the emotional actor who identifies with a role. Empathy makes an actor give very unequal performances: "full of fire at the first performance, he would be worn out and cold as marble at the third." On the other hand, the actor who acts cold-bloodedly would always be at his best, because he would be working artfully. Where Brecht parted company with Diderot, however, was in the ultimate *goal* of such rational acting. The Encyclopedist believed that the purpose of a cool performance is to counterfeit emotion, the better to deceive the spectators and arouse in them emotions which the actors themselves do not feel.[1]

Georg Fuchs' *Revolution in the Theatre*, published in 1909, attacked the deep, "peep-box" stage and naturalistic settings, and emphasized the importance to the actor's art of movement and dance. He also promoted the audience as creative partner in the dramatic production and, like Meyerhold, wrote about the Japanese use of color to symbolize emotional states. Fuchs' slogan "Rethéâtraliser le théâtre!" became famous.[2]

There are also important similarities between Meyerhold's techniques and those of the English director, designer, and theoretician Gordon Craig. Indeed the two men were friends, praised each other's work, and began to formulate their ideas about the same time. In an essay written about 1930, Craig made the following comparisons between Russian and English avant-garde theater:

London may expect to be told through the press how all theater ideas came streaming from Russia, and that Moscow is the very cradle of ideas. Believe me, London need not bother to believe this. . . . The talent of the Russian is great, but it is the talent for annexation of ideas . . . to which he then applies his technique. . . .

It will come as a shock to a number of critics to find that in praising Moscow's latest theaters they have been praising the ideas of Craig. . . . And we can congratulate all actors and artists of Russia on having advanced to at any rate a point to which our theater has not advanced, thanks to my detractors.

Craig's discussion of Meyerhold, whom he called "a technical artist of immense ability," included the ironically prophetic observation that "it is, of course, rather hard on [Meyerhold] to threaten him that if he doesn't produce plays red enough he will be shot—that is, I take it, the position in which poor Meyerhold is placed . . . but he seems to thrive."[3]

In 1919 Leopold Jessner (1878–1945) took over the leadership of the National Theater in Berlin. His productions were distin-

guished by highly abstract settings, his famous hallmark, a set
of steps dominating the stage. Samuel and Thomas believe that
Jessner invented this device, which "gives the impression of
filling the stage and dividing it into a number of vertical sections."[4] Other critics derive the stage staircase from Craig and
the Swiss Adolphe Appia. In 1907, however, Russian theater
critics were very much impressed by the broad staircase "extending the full width of the stage from the line of the proscenium arch to the back wall," which Meyerhold created for his
production of Sologub's *Death's Victory*. Meyerhold would have
liked to extend the steps into the auditorium, the better to "break
the barrier of the footlights and establish a more direct relationship between performer and spectator."[5]

In general, Expressionist productions such as Jessner's featured settings which tried to reflect essence rather than outward
reality by using a single dominant object: an arch, a gallows, a
chair, or the like, of exaggerated proportions. The stylistic parallels are obvious in Meyerhold's work, more muted in Brecht's.
Writing in 1925, Jessner remarked that revolutionary changes in
German theater had been surpassed only by the "unchained"
theater of Tairov and Meyerhold, which had pushed far beyond
the borders of its own country. He also defended Meyerhold's
and Tairov's aggressive text adaptations.[6]

Certainly Jessner's dramas had marked similarities to Meyerholdian theater: weird costumes, garish wigs, masked faces,
puppet-like movements. The former also used the style of the
Moritat (a folk ballad about a gruesome event), as did Brecht in
The Threepenny Opera and *The Life of Edward II of England*. Brecht
saw such ballads performed at fairs in Augsburg. Meyerhold,
in a 1913 essay on folk theater, also recommended as a dramatic
model this type of naive performance.

The Expressionist theater "The Tribune," founded in 1919,
"abolished the barrier between stage and auditorium and created
a unity of actors and public."[7] But despite the obvious stylistic
parallels between Expressionist and epic theater, there was an
important difference between them. Expressionism was subjec-
tive, heavily emotional, often bombastic in style (hence the term
"O-Mensch" drama), and the hero was perceived as an isolated
Self, rather than as an interacting part of a larger social group.[8]

Though born in Russia, Meyerhold shared with Brecht the cultural milieu which nurtured German Expressionism. Both were raised in prosperous middle-class German households, supported by fathers who made their living in business, and who (vainly) envisioned for their clever sons a university education which would lead to a respectable remunerative career as doctor or lawyer. As a first-generation Russian born to German parents, Meyerhold was very close to the cultural heritage into which Brecht was born and educated. As a director of Wagnerian opera, he may have known more than Brecht about that aspect of German dramatic art.

During most of Meyerhold's life, travel between East and West was easy and frequent. There existed a brilliant international community of innovative artists and critics, a community which did not reappear after 1933. Norris Houghton wrote in the 1930s that just as once all roads led to Rome "today, . . . in the theater, . . . the road leads to Moscow."[9] And the leader of the Moscow dramatic avant-garde was Meyerhold. So it is not surprising that many considered Meyerhold to be a fountainhead of new ideas in the theater and attributed to him the authorship of techniques which others such as Brecht and Piscator used to great advantage. Then came the period of Hitler and Stalin.

Meyerhold was officially "rehabilitated" in 1955, and his reputation slowly began to reestablish itself. People who had known him were once again able to write about him and to describe his work. Some of his archives were made available to Soviet and foreign researchers, and four volumes of his writings (including letters) have been published in the Soviet Union.

It has been the purpose of this monograph to shed some light on the problem of the relationship between the work of Brecht and Meyerhold by showing what the avenues and opportunities of contact were and by comparing the most important elements of their theory and practice. Brecht's contacts with Meyerhold's theater were many and varied, and occasionally direct. It would have been difficult, perhaps impossible, for Brecht not to have known that by the late twenties Meyerhold had brought to fruition a dramatic style which was still, as Bernhard Reich put it, Brecht's *Wunschideal*. Differences in their dramatic theories are insignificant. In the matter of practice, the differences lie in the area of experimental range; there is hardly any device used by Brecht or his acknowledged mentor Piscator which had not been tried first by Meyerhold. On the other hand, though Brecht used the treadmill as an epic technique, he seems not to have been interested in the thrust stage, vertically and horizontally moving platforms, and "active" scenery. Nor did Brecht share Meyerhold's profound interest in the problem of constructing a theater building which would, through its architecture, help to realize certain important esthetic and social principles.

Brecht's and Meyerhold's theories accord well with their practice, and even the early theories harmonize with the later plays and productions. Perhaps this is because both dramatists were adept at describing their own work and the larger meaning that work held for them. Their social theories of theater were also flexible enough, as they themselves pointed out, to embrace a wide variety of methods and experiments.

The lives and careers of the two theater workers continued to intertwine even after their deaths, when Brecht's plays and dramatic theories became the "Trojan horse"[10] by which Meyerholdian ideas were smuggled back into the Soviet Union in the 1950s. In 1964 the Moscow Taganka Theater staged as its first production Brecht's *The Good Person of Sezuan*, under the direction of Iuri Liubimov (who later became an exile in the West). In many ways that production synthesized the best in the currents of the old and the new avant-garde. The actors were products of the Vakhtangov school, a school deeply influenced by both Stanislavsky and Meyerhold. The "inventive and daring" production style was based on nearly forgotten traditions of Meyerholdian theater: the bare stage and brick backstage wall, simple props (student desks) which symbolized a wide variety of objects and settings, fast scene changes, and the use of mime, dance, and music as elements of theatrical montage. But this was not an imitative production. It was both a "restoration" and a "re-interpretation" of the best of Russian experimental theater.[11] The Taganka theater flourished for twenty years, until Liubimov was expelled from his theater and his country. Perhaps Meyerhold's face suddenly became too visible behind the mask of the troublesome, "classic" Brecht.

In the West, the innovations which Meyerhold pioneered and

Brecht kept lively are still developing and still controversial. For example, when Meyerhold called for audience participation, he meant intellectual participation which was orchestrated by the director and performers.

In recent years the idea that audience, playwright, and actors ought to be co-creators of a performance has sometimes been extended to include actual vocal and physical audience participation, regardless of whether all the members of the audience are ready or willing to join in. In certain experimental productions actors and actresses have invaded the private world of the audience. The spectator was invited to join the actors onstage, or the actors, with an "embrace" or "assault," invaded the spectator's territory. Spectators felt uncomfortable; some became so intensely embarrassed that they left the theater rather than continue as "actors." This aggressiveness toward the playgoer, an attempt to unify the world of the audience and the world of the players, parallels Meyerhold's and Brecht's theory of the creative audience.[12]

Contemporary popular criticism still attacks directors who play fast and loose with texts. With the opening of Andrei Serban's *Agamemnon*, the *New York Times* critic Walter Kerr declared that he had no quarrel with "visual techniques" as long as they remained subordinate to the "all-important text." He objected strongly to the use of classic texts as vehicles for formal experimentation by the director, and to directors who do not "respect" the playwright's words. Kerr attacked Serban's reworking of *Agamemnon* with the same phrases Soviet critics once used to blast such Meyerhold productions as *The Inspector General*, *Woe to Wit*, and *The Forest*. In fact, his account of Serban's production sounds like a description of Meyerhold's shows.

What Aeschylus wrote in the "Agamemnon" is deliberately, resolutely buried beneath dumb-show, processional, torchlight spectacle throughout.

For [Serban's] thrust, like the central thrust of almost all the experimentation directly preceding him, is primarily visual, profoundly *theatrical* rather than literary, derived not so much from the word as from the circus, from pantomime and *commedia dell' arte*, from gymnastics and religious ritual, from painting and revue and Grand Guignol, from dance. In the sense that these things are always given precedence, our avant-garde is anti-text, anti-literary. In the sense that dramatic logic and dramatic psychology have been superseded by theatrical spectacle, it is also anti-intellectual.[13]

The historical paradox lies in the charge that what all this adds up to is theater which is essentially anti-intellectual. Soviet and East German critics who in the 1920s and 1930s objected to Meyerhold's and Brecht's use of the same sort of visual devices and who thought they made too free with classic texts, almost always concluded with the damaging observation that such theater was too intellectual and (consequently) of no interest to "the masses."[14]

Such criticisms fail to recognize that art by its nature breeds fantasy, grotesquerie, and innovation. No Trojan horse, Brechtian or otherwise, is really needed to sneak these devices into the citadel and no city gates, no matter how well fortified, can keep imagination out forever.

NOTES

1. Denis Diderot, *The Paradox of Acting* (New York: Hill and Wang, 1957), pp. 14–15, 19–20, 22–23, 26.

2. Georg Fuchs, *Revolution in the Theater: Conclusions Concerning the Munich Artist's Theatre*, condensed and adapted by Constance C. Kuhn (1909; Ithaca, N.Y.: Cornell University Press, 1959), pp. 33, 39–41, 50–51, 90–91, 99. "Fuchs helped Meyerhold by giving him a theoretical justification for what he was already attempting to do" (Robert C. Williams, *Artists in Revolution: Portraits of the Russian Avant-Garde, 1905–1925* [Bloomington: Indiana University Press, 1977], p. 95).

3. Gordon Craig, "New Book and Old Memories" [review of René Fülop-Miller's and Paul Gregor's *The Russian Theater with Special Reference to the Revolution*], *The Boston Transcript* (April 26, 1930?): 4,6.

4. Richard Samuel and R. Hinton Thomas, *Expressionism in German Life, Literature, and the Theatre (1910–1924)*, 1st American ed. (Philadelphia: Albert Saifer, 1971), p. 67.

5. Edward Braun, ed. and trans., *Meyerhold on Theatre* (New York: Hill and Wang, 1969), p. 22.

6. Leopold Jessner, *Schriften. Theater der zwanziger Jahre*, ed. Hugo Fetting (Berlin: Henschelverlag Kunst und Gesellschaft, 1979), pp. 159–60, 162–63.

7. Richard Samuel and R. Hinton Thomas, *Expressionism in German*

124 Theater of Meyerhold and Brecht

Life, Literature, and the Theater (1910–1924), 1st American ed. (Philadelphia: Albert Saifer, 1971), pp. 66–68; J. M. Ritchie, *German Expressionist Drama* (Boston: Twayne, 1976), p. 38; Marjorie L. Hoover, "Meyerhold—To the West All New," paper read at the annual meeting of the American Association for the Advancement of Slavic Studies, Columbus, Ohio, October 13, 1978.

8. John Gassner, *Form and Idea in Modern Theater* (New York: Dryden Press, 1956), pp. 117, 120–29.

9. Norris Houghton, *Moscow Rehearsals*, 2d ed. (New York: Grove Press, 1962), p. xi.

10. See Henry Glade, "Major Brecht Productions in the Soviet Union since 1957," in *Bertolt Brecht: Political Theory and Literary Practice*, ed. Betty Nance Weber and Hubert Heinen (Athens: The University of Georgia Press, 1980), p. 89.

11. Konstantin Rudnitsky, "The Lessons Learned from Brecht," *Theatre Research International* 6 (Winter 1980/81): 62–72.

12. Helene Keysser, "I Love You. Who Are You? The Strategy of Drama in Recognition Scenes," *PMLA* 92 (March 1977): 297.

13. "The New Theater Is All Show," *New York Times*, "Theater," 12 June 1977, p. 3.

14. Bernhard Reich, "Meyerholds neue Inszenierung," *Die literarische Welt* (Berlin), 18 (1928); see also his "Dramaturgicheskaia kontseptsiia Meierkhol'da," *Oktiabr'* (1934): 242–48.

BIBLIOGRAPHY

Many of Meyerhold's theoretical writings and pronouncements have been translated into English by Edward Braun in *Meyerhold on Theatre*. Many of Brecht's theoretical writings are available in English in John Willett's translations: *Brecht on Theatre* and *The Messingkauf Dialogues*. English translations of Brecht's plays are listed in the bibliography to Ronald Hayman's *Brecht*, p. 408.

Abensour, Gérard. "Art et politique: La tournée du Théâtre Meyerhold à Paris en 1930." *Cahiers du monde Russe et Soviétique* 17 (April-September 1976): 213–48.

Alpers, Boris. *Teatr sotsial'noi maski.* Moscow-Leningrad: Gos. izd. khud. lit., 1931. English title: *The Theater of the Social Mask.* Translated by Mark Schmidt. New York: Group Theater, 1934.

Angres, Dora. *Die Beziehungen Lunačrskijs zur deutschen Literatur.* Berlin: Akademie-Verlag, 1970.

Arbenina, Stella. *Through Terror to Freedom.* London: Hutchinson, 1929(?).

Aubry, Yves. "Slatan Dudow, 1903–1961." *Anthologie du cinéma* 6 (1971): 387–440.

Bab, Julius. *Das Theater der Gegenwart: Geschichte der dramatischen Bühne seit 1870.* Leipzig: Verlagsbuchhandlung von J. J. Weber, 1928.

Bakshy, Alexander. *The Path of the Modern Russian Stage, and Other Essays.* London: Cecil Palmer & Hayward, 1916.

Balász, Béla. "Meyerhold und Stanislawsky." *Das Wort* 5 (May 1938): 115–21.

Baxandall, Lee. "Brecht in America, 1935." *The Drama Review* 12 (Fall 1967): 69–87.

Bechterev, V. M. *General Principles of Human Reflexology.* Translated by Emma and William Murphy. New York: 1932. Reprint. New York: Arno Press, 1973.

Beckley, Richard. "Adaptation as a Feature of Brecht's Dramatic Technique." *German Life and Letters* 15 (July 1962): 274–84.

Benjamin, Walter. *Briefe* Edited by Gershom Scholem and Theodor W. Adorno. Frankfurt a.M.: Suhrkamp, 1966.

————. *Moskauer Tagebuch.* Edited by Gershom Scholem. Frankfurt a.M.: Suhrkamp, 1980.

————. "Programm eines proletarischen Kindertheaters." In *Revolutionär im Beruf.* By Anna Lacis. Edited by Hildegard Brenner. Munich: Rogner und Bernhard, 1971.

————. "Der Regisseur Meyerhold—in Moskau erledigt?" *Die literarische Welt* (11 February 1927): 3.

————. *Versuche über Brecht.* Frankfurt a.M.: Suhrkamp, 1966. English title: *Understanding Brecht.* Translated by Anna Bostock. London: NLB, 1973.

Bentley, Eric. "Introduction." In *Seven Plays by Bertolt Brecht.* New York: Grove Press, 1961.

Berg-Pan, Renata. "Mixing Old and New Wisdom: The 'Chinese' Sources of Brecht's *Kaukasischer Kreidedreis and Other Works.*" *The Germanic Quarterly* 48 (March 1975): 204–28.

Berlau, Ruth, et al. *Theaterarbeit: 6 Aufführungen des Berliner Ensembles.* 2d revised and enlarged edition. Berlin: Henschelverlag Kunst und Gesellschaft, 1961.

"Bert Brekht v. Moskve." *Pravda* (23 April 1935): 4.

"Bertolt Brecht und die sowjetische Kunst und Literatur." In *Geschichte der russischen Sowjetliteratur 1917–1941.* Edited by Harri Jünger. Berlin: Akademie-Verlag, 1973, pp. 610–11.

Blum, Oscar. "Russische Theaterköpfe. II: Meyerhold." *Die Weltbühne* (22 June 1926): 265.

Blum, W. "Die neue russische Dramaturgie." *Das neue Russland* (1925): 26–28.

Bojko, Szymon. *New Graphic Design in Revolutionary Russia.* New York: Praeger, 1972.

Braun, Edward, editor and translator. *Meyerhold on Theatre.* New York: Hill and Wang, 1969.

————. *The Theatre of Meyerhold: Revolution on the Modern Stage.* New York: Drama Book Specialists, 1979.

Brecht, Bertolt. *Edward II: A Chronicle Play.* Translated by Eric Bentley. New York: Grove Press, 1966.

————. *Gesammelte Werke.* Frankfurt a.M.: Suhrkamp, 1967.

————. "Ist das Volk unfehlbar?"; "Rat an Tretjakow, Gesund zu werden." In *Gedichte.* Vol. 5, *1934–1941.* Frankfurt a.M.: Suhrkamp, 1964.

————. *The Messingkauf Dialogues.* Edited and translated by John Willett. London: Methuen, 1965.

————. *Schriften zum Theater*. Edited by Werner Hecht. Frankfurt a.M.: Suhrkamp, 1963–1967.

————. "Über reimlose Lyrik mit unregelmässigen Rhythmen." In *Versuche*. Vol. 12. Frankfurt a.m.: Suhrkamp, 1958.

"Brecht-Eisler." *International Literature* (1932): 157–58.

Brown, Edward J. "The Formalist Contribution." *The Russian Review* 33 (July 1974): 243–58.

Brüggemann, Heinz. "Tretjakov und Brecht." In *Literarische Technik und soziale Revolution*. Reinbek bei Hamburg: Rowohlt, 1973.

Canaris, Volker. *Leben Eduards des Zweiten von England als vormarxistisches Stück Bertolt Brechts*. Bonn: Bouvier, 1973.

Chistowa, Bella. "Wladimir Majakowskijs Beziehungen zu deutschen Literaturschaffenden." *Kunst und Literatur* 9 (1961).

Craig, Edward Gordon. "New Book and Old Memories." In *The Boston Transcript* (26 April 1930?): 4, 6.

————. *On the Art of the Theatre*. London: 1911. Reprint. New York: Theatre Arts Books, 1957.

DeGeorge, Fernande M. "From Russian Formalism to French Structuralism." *Comparative Literature Studies* 14 (March 1977): 20–29.

Deutscher, Isaac. "Introduction" to A. V. Lunacharsky's *Revolutionary Silhouettes*. Translated by Michael Glenny. London: The Penguin Press, 1967.

Diderot, Denis. *Paradoxe sur le comédien*. Paris, 1773–78; English title: *The Paradox of Acting*. New York: Hill and Wang, 1957.

Dombrow, Sinclair. "The Russian Renaissance in Berlin." *Shadowland* (June 1923): 22–24, 73.

"The Dramatist and His Theme." *International Literature* 2 (1933): 139–40.

Düwel, Gudrun. "Zur Bedeutung der Oktoberrevolution und der Sowjetliteratur für die deutsche sozialistische Literatur bis 1945." In *Begegnung und Bündnis*. Edited by Gerhard Ziegengeist. Berlin: Akademie-Verlag, 1972.

Ehrenburg, Ilya. *Men, Years, Life*. Vol. 3: *Truce: 1921–1933*. Translated by Tatania Shebunina and Yvonne Kapp. London: Macgibbon, 1936. Also published as *Memoirs: 1921–1941*. New York: Grosset & Dunlap, 1966.

Erpenbeck, Fritz. "Nachwort" to the reprinted edition of *Das Wort*. Zurich: Limmat, 1968.

Etkind, Efim. "Brecht and the Soviet Theater." In *Bertolt Brecht: Political Theory and Literary Practice*. Edited by Betty Nance Weber and Hubert Heinen. Athens: University of Georgia Press, 1980.

Fedorov, V. "Masterskaia Meierkhol'da." *Lef* 2 (April-May 1923): 170–72.

128   Bibliography

Fevral'skii, A. V. "S. M. Tret'iakov v teatre Meierkhol'da." in *Slyshish'*, *Moskva?!* By Sergei M. Tret'iakov. Moscow: Iskusstvo, 1966.

Fiebach, Joachim. "Beziehungen zwischen dem sowjetischen und dem proletarisch-revolutionären Theater der Weimarer Republik." In *Deutschland. Sowjetunion.* Edited by Heinz Sanke. Berlin: Humboldt University, 1966.

Fitzpatrick, Sheila. "A. V. Lunacharsky: Recent Soviet Interpretations and Republications." *Soviet Studies* 18 (January 1967): 267–89.

———. *The Commissariat of Enlightenment: Soviet Organization of the Arts under Lunacharsky: October 1917–1921.* Cambridge: Cambridge University Press, 1970.

Flanagan, Hallie. "Ivan as Critic." *Theatre Guild Magazine* 4 (January 1930): 40–42.

Fradkin, Ilja. *Bertolt Brecht: Weg und Methode.* Leipzig: Philipp Reclam jun., 1974.

Frank, Rudolf. *Spielzeit meines Lebens.* Heidelberg: L. Schneider, 1960.

Frioux, C. "Lunacharskij et le futurisme Russe." *Cahiers du monde Russe et Soviétique* 1 (January-March 1960): 307–18.

Fuchs, Georg. *Revolution in the Theatre: Conclusions Concerning the Munich Artist's Theatre (Die Revolution des Theaters).* Condensed and adapted by Constance Connor Kuhn. Munich: 1909. Reprint. Ithaca, N.Y.: Cornell University Press, 1959.

Fuegi, John. " 'The Caucasian Chalk Circle' in Performance." In *Brecht Heute. Brecht Today.* Vol. 1. Edited by Reinhold Grimm et al. Frankfurt a.M.: Athenäum, 1971.

———. *The Essential Brecht.* Los Angeles: Hennessey and Ingalls, 1972.

———. "Feuchtwanger, Brecht, and the 'Epic' Media the Novel and Film." In *Lion Feuchtwanger: Critical Essays.* Los Angeles: Hennessey and Ingalls, 1972.

———. "Russian 'Epic Theatre' Experiments and the American Stage." *The Minnesota Review,* New Series 1 (Fall 1973): 102–12.

———. "Slavic and Western Literary Theories in Contact." In *Yearbook of Comparative and General Literature.* (1972): 57–64.

Garin, Erast. *S Meierkhold'dom: Vospominaniia.* Moscow: Iskusstvo, 1974.

Gassner, John. *Form and Idea in Modern Theater.* New York: Holt, Rinehart and Winston, 1956.

Gerould, Daniel. "Russian Symbolist Drama and the Visual Arts." *Newsnotes on Soviet and East European Drama and Theatre* 4 (March 1984): 10–17.

Glade, Henry. "Major Brecht Productions in the Soviet Union since 1957." In *Bertolt Brecht: Political Theory and Literary Practice.* Edited by Betty Nance Weber and Hubert Heinen. Athens: University of Georgia Press, 1980.

Globig, Klaus. "Die Zeitschrift *Das neue Russland* als Propagandist der jungen Sowjetliteratur in Deutschland." in *Deutschland. Sowjetunion.* Edited by Heinz Sanke. Berlin: Humboldt University, 1966.

Gogol, Nikolai. *The Government Inspector.* Translated by J. D. Campbell. Foreward by Janko Lavrin. London: Wm. Heinemann, 1953.

Goldfarb, Alvin. "*Roar China* in a Nazi Concentration Camp." *Theatre Survey* 21 (November 1980): 184–85.

Gorchakov, Nikolai A. *The Theater in Soviet Russia.* Translated by Edgar Lehrman. New York: Columbia University Press, 1957.

Gorelik, Mordecai. "Brecht: 'I Am the Einstein of the New Stage Form . . .' " *Theatre Arts* 41 (March 1957): 72.

————. "Rational Theater." In *Brecht Heute. Brecht Today.* Vol. 1. Edited by Reinhold Grimm et al. Frankfurt a.M.: Athenäum, 1971.

Graf, Oskar Maria. "Briefe Sergej Tretjakows an Oskar Maria Graf." In *Reise in der Sowjetunion 1934.* Darmstadt und Neuwied: Luchterhand, 1974.

Gray, Camilla. *The Russian Experiment in Art: 1863–1922.* 2d edition. New York: Harry N. Abrams, 1970.

Grimm, Reinhold, ed. *B. Brecht. Leben Eduards des Zweiten von England: Vorlage, Texte und Materialien.* Frankfurt a.M.: Suhrkamp, 1968.

————. *Bertolt Brecht.* 3d revised edition. Stuttgart: J. B. Metzler, 1971.

————. "Piscator auf dem Streckbett." In *Brecht-Jahrbuch 1978.* Edited by Reinhold Grimm et al. Frankfurt a.M.: Suhrkamp, 1978.

Grüninger, Hans Werner. "Brecht und Marlowe." *Comparative Literature Studies* 21 (Summer 1969): 232–44.

Guilbeaux, Henri. "Meyerhold et les tendances du théâtre contemporain." *Les Humbles* 15 (May-June 1930): 3–40.

Gyseghem, André van. *Theater in Soviet Russia.* London: Faber and Faber, 1943.

Hayman, Ronald. *Brecht: A Biography.* New York: Oxford University Press, 1983.

Hecht, Werner, ed. *Materialien zu Brechts "Der kaukasische Kreidedreis."* 2d edition. Frankfurt a.M.: Suhrkamp, 1968.

Hill, Claude. *Bertolt Brecht.* Boston: Twayne 1975.

Hoffmann, Ludwig, and Daniel Hoffman-Otwald. "Das Gastpiel der Moskauer blauen Bluse in Deutschland 1927." In *Deutsches Arbeitertheater 1918–1933.* Vol. 1. Munich: Rogner und Bernhard, 1973.

Holitscher, Arthur. "Drei Monate in Sowjet-Russland." *Die neue Rundschau* (January 1921): 1–32, 121–63, 236–62.

Holter, Howard Ralph. "A. V. Lunacharsky and the Formulation of a Policy toward the Arts in the RSFSR 1921–1927." Ph.D. diss., University of Wisconsin, 1967.

————. "The Legacy of Lunacharsky and Artistic Freedom in the USSR." *Slavic Review* 29 (1970): 262–82.

Hoover, Marjorie L. "Brecht's Soviet Connection: Tretiakov." In *Brecht Heute. Brecht Today.* Vol. 3. Edited by Gisela Bahr et al. Frankfurt a.M.: Athenäum, 1973.

————. "A Mejerxol'd Method?—*Love for Three Oranges* (1914–1916)." *Slavic and East European Journal* 13 (1969): 23–41.

————. *Meyerhold: The Art of Conscious Theater.* Amherst: University of Massachusetts Press, 1974.

————. "V. E. Meyerhold: A Russian Predecessor of Avant-Garde Theater." *Comparative Literature* 17 (Summer 1965): 234–50.

Houghton, Norris. *Moscow Rehearsals.* 2d edition. New York: Grove Press, 1962.

————. *Return Engagement.* London: Putnam, 1962.

————. "Theory into Practice: A Reappraisal of Meierhold." *Educational Theatre Journal* 20 (October 1968): 437–42.

Huppert, Hugo. "Das Taubenhaus." *Neue Deutsche Literatur* 20 (December 1972): 6–34.

Hurwicz, Angelika. *Brecht inszeniert: "Der kaukasische Kreidedreis."* Velber bei Hannover: Friedrich, 1964.

Ihering, Herbert. *Von Reinhardt bis Brecht.* Berlin: Aufbau-Verlag, 1959.

Innes, C. D. *Erwin Piscator's Political Theatre: The Development of Modern German Drama.* Cambridge: Cambridge University Press, 1972.

Jessner, Leopold. *Schriften: Theater der zwanziger Jahre.* Edited by Hugo Fetting. Berlin: Henschelverlag Kunst und Gesellschaft, 1979.

Kesting, Marianne. *Entdeckung und Destruktion: Zur Strukturumwandlung der Künste.* Munich: Wilhelm Fink, 1970.

————. "Wagner/Meyerhold/Brecht oder die Erfindung des 'epischen' Theaters." In *Brecht-Jahrbuch 1977.* Edited by Reinhold Grimm et al. Frankfurt a.M.: Suhrkamp, 1977.

Keyssar, Helene. "I Love You. Who Are You? The Strategy of Drama in Recognition Scenes." *PMLA* 92 (March 1977): 297–306.

Knopf, Jan. *Bertolt Brecht. Ein kritischer Forschungsbericht: Fragwürdiges in der Brecht-Forschung.* Frankfurt a.M.: Athenäum, 1974.

Knust, Herbert. "Piscator and Brecht: Affinity and Alienation." In *Essays on Brecht: Theater and Politics.* Edited by Siegfried Mews and Herbert Knust. Chapel Hill: University of North Carolina Press, 1974.

Kopelev, Lev. *Brekht.* Moscow: Molodaia gvardiia, 1966. See also, Kopelew.

Kopelew, Lew. "Brecht und die russische Theaterrevolution." In *Brecht Heute. Brecht Today.* Vol. 3. Edited by Gisela Bahr et al. Frankfurt a.M.: Athenäum, 1973. See also, Kopelev.

Kreilisheim, Eva. "Bertolt Brecht und die Sowjetunion." Ph.D. diss., University of Vienna, 1969.

Kussmaul, Paul. *Bertolt Brecht und das Englisches Drama der Renaissance.* Bern and Frankfurt: Herbert Lang, 1974.

Kuz'min, M. S. "Obrazovanie v Germanii obshchestva druzei novoi Rossii." In *Vestnik Leningradskogo Universiteta* 1(1962): 150–55.

Lachmann, Renate. "Die 'Verfremdung' und das 'Neue Sehen' bei Viktor Šklovskij." *Poetica* 3 (1970): 226–49.

Lacis, Anna. "Bert Brekht." *Sovetskii teatr* 6 (1932): 27–29.

————. *Revoliutsionnyi teatr Germanii.* Translated from German mss. by N. Barkhash. Moscow: 1935.

————. *Revolutionär im Beruf: Berichte über proletarisches Theater, über Meyerhold, Brecht, Benjamin, und Piscator.* Edited by Hildegard Brenner. Munich: Rogner und Bernhard, 1971.

Ley-Piscator, Maria. *The Piscator Experiment: The Political Theater.* New York: J. Heineman, 1967.

Lissitzky, El. *Exhibit.* Cologne: Galerie Gmurzynska, 1976.

Lozowick, Louis. "V. E. Meyerhold and His Theatre." *The Hound and Horn* 4 (October-December 1930): 95–105.

Lunacharskaia-Rozenel', Nataliia A. *Pamiat' serdtsa: Vospominaniia.* Moscow: 1962.

Lunacharskii, Anatolii V. "Na tri grosha." In *O teatre i dramaturgii.* Vol. 2. Moscow: Iskusstvo, 1958.

————. "Die neue Dramaturgie." *Das neue Russland* (1926): 9–10.

————. *On Literature and Art.* 2d revised edition. Moscow: Progress Publishers, 1973.

————. *Sobranie Sochinenii.* Vols. 3 and 6. Moscow: Khudozhestvennaia literatura, 1964, 1965.

Lyon, James K. "Der Briefwechsel zwischen Bertolt Brecht und der New Yorker Theatre Union von 1935." In *Brecht-Jahrbuch 1975.* Edited by Reinhold Grimm et al. Frankfurt a.M.: Suhrkamp, 1975.

McDowell, W. Stuart. "Actors on Brecht: The Munich Years." *The Drama Review* 20 (September 1976): 101–16.

Mailand-Hansen, Christian. *Mejerchol'ds Theaterästhetik in den 1920er Jahren.* Copenhagen: Rosenkilde und Bagger, 1980.

Mann, Thomas. "German Letter." *The Dial* 77 (November 1924): 414–19.

Markov, Pavel. *The Soviet Theatre.* London: V. Gollancz, 1934.

Marlowe, Christopher. *Edward II.* Edited by H. B. Charlton and R. D. Waller. 2d revised edition. London: Methuen, 1955.

Marshall, Herbert. *The Pictorial History of the Russian Theatre.* New York: Crown, 1977.

Mayakovsky, Vladimir. *The Complete Plays of Vladimir Mayakovsky.* Translated by Guy Daniels. New York: Washington Square Press, 1968.

Meierkhol'd, Vesvolod E. *Perepiska*. Moscow: Iskusstvo, 1976.
————. *Stat'i, Pis'ma, Rechi, Besedy*. Moscow: Iskusstvo, 1968.
————. *Tvorcheskoe nasledie V. E. Meierkhol'da*. Edited by L. D. Vendrovskaia and A. V. Fevral'skii. Moscow: Vseross. teatr. obsh., 1978.
Meserve, Walter and Ruth. "The Stage History of *Roar, China!*: Documentary Drama as Propaganda." *Theatre Survey* 21 (May 1980): 1–13.
Mierau, Fritz. *Erfindung und Korrektur. Tretjakows Ästhetik der Operativität*. Berlin: Akademie-Verlag, 1976.
————. "Polemik und Korrespondenz: Fjodor Gladkow und Sergei Tretjakow." *Weimarer Beiträge* (December 1973): 66–81.
————. "Die Rezeption der sowjetischen Literatur in Deutschland 1920–24." *Zeitschrift für Slawistik* 3 (1958): 620–38.
————. "Tatsache und Tendenz: (Teil I). Der Schriftsteller Sergej Tretjakow." *Weimarer Beiträge* 19 (1972): 66–97.
Murav'ev, Iurii P. "Sovetsko-germanskie sviazi v oblasti literary i iskusstva v gody Veimarskoi respubliki." In *Slaviano-germanskie kul'turnye sviazi i otnosheniia*. General editor, V. D. Koroliuk. Moscow: Nauka, 1969.
Nakov, Andrei B. *Russian Pioneers: At the Origins of Non-Objective Art*. London: Annely P. Juda Fine Art, 1976.
Niessen, Carl. *Brecht auf der Bühne*. Cologne: Institut für Theaterwissenschaft an der Universität Köln, 1959.
Norris, Faith G. "The Collaboration of Lion Feuchtwanger and Bertolt Brecht." *Lion Feuchtwanger: Critical Essays*. Los Angeles: Hennessey and Ingalls, 1972.
Olesha, Iurii. "Meyerhold: Soviet Director. On His Sixtieth Birthday." *International Literature* 3 (1934): 137–38.
————. "Notes of a Writer." *International Literature* 3 (1934): 148–51.
Pachaly, Erhard, et al. "Die kulturelle Beziehungen zwischen Deutschland und der Sowjetunion." *Die grosse sozialistische Octoberrevolution und Deutschland*. Vol. 1. Edited by Alfred Anderle et al. Berlin: Dietz, 1967.
Petzet, Wolfgang. *Theater: Die Münchner Kammerspiele, 1911–1972*. Munich: Kurt Desch, 1973.
Pike, David. *German Writers in Soviet Exile, 1933–1945*. Chapel Hill: University of North Carolina Press, 1982.
Piscator, Erwin. *Das politische Theater*. Facsimile of 1st edition, 1929. Berlin: Henschelverlag, 1968.
Reich, Bernhard. "Dramaturgicheskaia kontseptsiia Meierkhol'da." *Oktiabr'* (1934): 242–48.
————. "Meyerholds neue Inszenierung." *Die literarische Welt* 18 (1928).

―――. "O sovremennikom nemetskom teatre." *Pechat' i revoliutsiia* 2 (1926).

―――. "Sovremennaia nemetskaia dramaturgiia." *Novyi mir* 5 (1926): 159–61.

―――. *Im Wettlauf mit der Zeit: Erinnerungen aus fünf Jahrzehnten deutscher Theatergeschichte.* Berlin: Henschelverlag, 1970. Russian adaptation: *Vena-Berlin-Moskva-Berlin.* Moscow: Iskusstvo, 1972.

Ritchie, J. M. *German Expressionist Drama.* Boston: Twayne, 1976.

Rodyenko, Peter. "Napoleon in Shanghai: A Russian Designer's Waterloo." *Theatre Arts Monthly* 17 (April 1933): 298–306.

Rosenbauer, Hansjürgen. *Brecht und der Behaviorismus.* Bad Homburg: Gehlen, 1970.

Rudnitsky, Konstantin. "The Lessons Learned from Brecht." *Theatre Research International* 6 (Winter 1980/81): 62–72.

―――. *Meyerhold the Director.* Edited by Sydney Schultze. Ann Arbor, Mich.: Ardis, 1981.

Ruhle, Günther. *Theater für die Republik, 1917–1933: Im Spiegel der Kritik.* Frankfurt a.M.: Fischer, 1967.

Rülicke-Weiler, Käthe. *Die Dramaturgie Brechts: Theater als Mittel der Veränderung.* Berlin: Henschelverlag, 1966.

―――. " 'Since Then the World Has Hope': Brecht in the Soviet Union." In *Brecht as They Knew Him.* Edited by Hubert Witt, translated by John Peet. New York: International Publishers, 1974.

Samuel, Richard, and R. Hinton Thomas. *Expressionism in German Life, Literature, and the Theater (1910–1924).* 1st American edition. Philadelphia: Albert Saifer, 1971.

Saylor, Oliver. *Russian Theatre under the Revolution.* Boston: Little, Brown, 1920.

Schmidt, Paul, ed. *Meyerhold at Work.* Austin: University of Texas Press, 1980.

Schonauer, Franz. "Tretjakow und die neue Linke." *Neue Rundschau* (1972): 585–89.

Schumacher, Ernst and Renate. *Leben Brechts in Wort und Bild.* Berlin: Henschelverlag Kunst und Gesellschaft, 1978.

Scott, A. C. *Mei Lan-fang: Leader of the Pear Garden.* Hong Kong: Hong Kong University Press, 1959.

Seton, Marie. "Soviet Theatre Downstream." *Theatre Arts Monthly* 15 (December 1931): 1035–37.

Shklovsky, Viktor. "Art as Technique." In *Russian Formalist Criticism.* Translated by Lee T. Lemon and Marion J. Reis. 2d edition. Lincoln: University of Nebraska Press, 1969.

―――. *Mayakovsky and His Circle.* Edited and translated by Lily Feiler. New York: Dodd, Mead, 1972.

134 Bibliography

Singermann, Boris. "Brechts *Dreigroschenoper*. Zur Ästhetik der Montage." In *Brecht-Jahrbuch* 1976. Edited by R. Grimm et al. Frankfurt a.M.: Suhrkamp, 1976. See also, Zingerman.

Slonim, Marc. *Russian Theater*. New York: World, 1961.

Steinweg, Reiner. *Das Lehrstück: Brechts Theorie einer politisch-ästhetischen Erzeihung*. Stuttgart: J.B. Metzler, 1972.

Sternberg, Fritz. *Der Dichter und die Ratio: Erinnerungen an Bertolt Brecht*. Göttingen: Sachse und Pohl, 1963.

Szondi, Peter. *Theorie des modernen Dramas*. Frankfurt a.M.: Suhrkamp, 1956.

Tait, A. L. "Lunacharsky, the 'Poet-Commissar.' " *The Slavonic and East European Review* 52 (April 1974): 234–51.

Thun, Nyota. "Majakowski und Deutschland." *Neue Deutsche Literatur* 1 (July 1953): 158–73.

Tietze, Rosemarie, ed. *Vsevolod Meyerhold: Theaterarbeit 1917–1930*. Munich: Carl Hanser, 1974.

Tomashevsky, Boris. "Thematics." In *Russian Formalist Criticism*. Translated by Lee T. Lemon and Marion J. Reis. 2d edition. Lincoln: University of Nebraska Press, 1969.

Tret'iakov, Sergei M. *B. Brekht: Epicheskie dramy*. Moscow-Leningrad: 1934.

———. *A Chinese Testament: The Autobiography of Tan Shi-hua*. New York: Simon and Schuster, 1934.

———. "Dramaturg-Didakt. (O p'ese B. Brekhta 'Mat' ')." *Internatsionalnaia literatura* (1933): 116–118.

———. *Khochu rebenka* (Scenes 4 and 5). *Novyi LEF* 3 (1927): 3–11.

———. "Rech' S. M. Tret'iakova." *Pervyi vsesoiuznyi s'ezd sovetskikh pisatelei* (1934), pp. 344–46.

———. *Roar, China! An Episode in Nine Scenes*. Translated by F. Polianovskaia and Barbara Nixon. New York: International Publishers, 1931.

———. "Vsevolod Meierkohl'd." *LEF* (April-May 1923): 168–69. *See also*, Tretjakov; Tretjakow; Tretyakov.

Tretjakov, Sergej. *Die Arbeit des Schriftstellers*. Edited by Heiner Boehncke. Reinbek bei Hamburg: Rowohlt, 1972. *See also* Tret'iakov; Tretjakow; Tretyakov

Tretjakow, Sergej. *Feld-Herren: Der Kampf um eine Kollektivwirtschaft*. Translated by Rudolf Selke. Berlin: Malik-Verlag, 1931.

———. *Ich will ein Kind haben (Die Pionierin)*. Translated by Ernst Hube. Adapted by Bert Brecht. Freiburg im Breisgau: Max Reichard-Verlag, n.d.

———. *Ich will ein Kind haben* (first version). *Brülle, China!* Translated by Fritz Mierau. Berlin: Henschelverlag, 1976. *See also* Tret'iakov; Tretjakov; Tretyakov.

Tretyakov, Sergei. "Bert Brecht." In *International Literature* (May 1937): 60–70. *See also* Tret'iakov; Tretjakov; Tretjakow

Velekhova, N. *Ohklopkov i teatr ulitsa.* Moscow: Iskusstvo, 1970.

Vendrovskaia, L. D. *Vstrechi s Meierkhol'dom: Sbornik vospominanii.* Moscow: 1967.

Völker, Klaus. *Brecht: A Biography.* Translated by John Nowell. New York: Continuum, 1978.

———. *Brecht-Chronik: Daten zu Leben und Werk.* Munich: Carl Hanser, 1971.

Volkov, Nikolai D. *Meierkhol'd.* 2 vols. Moscow: 1926.

Weber, Carl. "Brecht as Director." *The Drama Review* 12 (Fall 1967): 101–7.

Weisstein, Ulrich. "The First Version of Brecht/Feuchtwanger's *Leben Eduards des Zweiten von England* and Its Relation to the Standard Text." *Journal of English and Germanic Philology* 69: 193–210.

———. "From the Dramatic Novel to Epic Theater: A Study of the Contemporary Background of Brecht's Theory and Practice." *The Germanic Review* 38 (May 1963): 257–71.

Wiese, Benno von. *Karl Immermann.* Bad Homburg: Dr. Max Gehlen, 1969.

Wilder, Harry. "Die 'Blauen Blusen' und wir." *Das Arbeitertheater* (1928): n.p.

Willett, John. *Brecht in Context: Comparative Approaches.* London and New York: Methuen, 1984.

———. *The Theatre of Bertolt Brecht: A Study from Eight Aspects.* New York: New Directions, 1968.

Williams, Robert C. *Artists in Revolution: Portraits of the Russian Avant-Garde.* Bloomington: Indiana University Press, 1977.

———. *Culture in Exile: Russian Emigres in Germany, 1881–1941.* Ithaca, N.Y.: Cornell University Press, 1972.

Zingerman, Boris. "Korifei sovetskoi rezhissury i mirovaia stsena." In *Voprosy teatra.* (1970): 86–108. See also, Singermann.

Zuckmayer, Carl. *A Part of Myself: Portrait of an Epoch.* Translated by Richard and Clara Winston. New York: Harcourt, 1970.

INDEX

Names mentioned in passing are not included. Titles appear under author's name.

Agitprop theater, German and Soviet, 36. *See also* Blue Blouse; TRAM

AIZ, (*"Arbeiter-Illustrierte Zeitung*), 12, 38 n.9

Alienation effect, 102-3. *See also Ostranenie; Otchuzhdenie;* V-Effect

Altenberg, Peter, 55

Andreev, Leonid: *The Life of a Man*, 53, 55; theory of "conscious" theater, 60

von Appen, Karl, 72 n.7

Appia, Adolphe, 119

Bab, Julius, 3, 6 n.10

Balasz, Bela, 36-37

Barthel, Max, 11-12

Bekhterev, Vladimir, 16, 17, 40-41, 64

Benjamin, Walter: comments on Tretiakov's *Field Marshals*, 27; conversation with Brecht about Expressionism-Realism debate, 99; in Moscow, 14-15, 18-19, 42 n.37, 77-78; writes about Lacis' children's theater, 17; writes about Meyerhold, 2, 19, 21, 89

Biberman, Herbert, 14

Blok, Aleksandr: *The Fairground Booth*, 52, 66, 103; *The Unknown Woman*, 53, 61

Blue Blouse theater, 13, 14, 32, 39 n.14

Brecht, Bertolt: on actors and acting, 64-65, 100-101, 118; alienation theories, 21, 35, 44 nn.47, 49, 102-3, 112 n.51; crowded setting, 81; epic theater, 1, 35, 36, 48, n.86, 76 n.75, 101-2; episode titles, 94; episodic structure, 92, 104, 113 n.58; film on stage, 68, 94, 96; and Formalism, 98, 102-3, 111 n.29; gestic acting, 35, 94; Gestus, 104-5; half curtain, 96-97; influence on Soviet literature and theater, 109; and A. Lacis, 18; lighting, 96, 108-9; and A.

V. Lunacharsky, 31-33; and Meyerhold, 1, 7 n.14, 13, 34-36, 46 n.76, 47-48 n.81; montage theater, 95-96, 103-4; in Moscow, 14-15, 21-23, 43 n.39, 47 n.79, 102; at the Munich-Kammerspiele, 17-18, 49, 91-95; music, 71, 94-96; new drama, 76 n.72; participatory audience, 103-4, 108; pictorial arrangements on stage, 98-99; settings, 72 n.7, 105-7; "social mask" theater, 107-8; and Soviet theater, 33-36, 49; text adaptation and reworking, 69-70, 91-93, 97-98; and Tretiakov, 20, 29, 43 n.43, 45 n.58; and Evgenii Vakhtangov, 35, 48 n.81; and Das Wort, 46-47 n.76. Works and productions: The Caucasian Chalk Circle, 24-26, 27, 28-30, 78, 93, 96, 99, 101-2, 104, 108; Drums in the Night, 15, 60, 114 n.66; Galileo (The Life of Galilei), 107, 114 n.71; The Good Person of Sezuan, 23, 27, 114 n.71, 121; Herr Puntila and His Servant Matti, 101, 107, 108, 111 n.34, 114 n.71; "Is the People Infallible?," 20; Katzgrabben (Erwin Strittmatter), 108; Kuhle Wampe, 15; The Life of Edward II of England (with L. Feuchtwanger), 17-18, 41-42 n.43, 49, 91-97, 110 n.15, 112 n.39, 119; Mahagonny, 68; A Man's a Man, 68, 78, 104; The Messingkauf Dialogues, 97, 100, 105; The Mother, 68, 105, 111 n.34; Mother Courage (Mother Courage and Her Children), 27, 71, 75 n.54, 96, 101-2, 107; The Pioneers of Ingolstadt, 3, 6 n.8;

The Resistible Rise of Arturo Ui, 104, 111 n.34; The Roundheads and the Peakheads, 78, 106; Schweyk in the Second World War, 104; The Threepenny Opera, 3, 32, 71, 75 n.47, 77, 96, 119
Brenck-Kalischer, Bess, 12

Calderòn de la Barca, Pedro: The Adoration of the Cross, 53, 55
Chaplin, Charlie, 66
Chekhov, Anton, 58, 62
Chekhov, Mikhail, 79-80
"Conscious" theater, 12. See also Brecht, alienation theories; Meyerhold, "conscious" theater
Constructivism, in theater, 72 n.7, 73 n.32, 78
Craig, Gordon, 63, 118, 119
Crommelynck, Fernand: The Magnanimous Cuckold, 11, 57, 65
Cubism, in theater, 10, 56, 73 n.32, 75 n.47, 106

Dessau, Paul, 96
Dialectic drama, 113 n.55. See also Brecht, epic theater, new drama; Tretiakov, dialectic drama
Diderot, Denis: Paradoxe sur le comédien, 117
Dudow, Slatan, 15, 40 n.21, 43 n.39
Dumas, Alexandre: Camille, 51, 53, 62

Ehrenburg, Ilya: Trust D. E., 11, 57, 68, 71, 77, 96, 106
Eisenstein, Sergei, 14, 41 n.22, 75 n.47, 102
Eisler, Hanns, 15

Entfremdung, 112 n.51

Epic theater, 35, 113 n.55, 114 n.7

Episodic structure, in drama. *See* Brecht, episodic structure; Meyerhold, episodic structure

Erpenbeck, Fritz, 46-47 n.76

Evreinov, Nikolai, 39 n.13

Expressionism: in theater, 106, 119; Expressionism vs. Realism debate, 99-100

Faiko, Alexei: *Teacher Bubus*, 11, 71

Falckenberg, Otto, 41-42 n.33, 60, 106, 114 n.66

Feuchtwanger, Lion, 46 n.76; *The Life of Edward II of England* (with Brecht), 18, 49, 91-93, 95

Flanagan, Hallie, 74 n.40

Fleisser, Marie-Luise: *The Pioneers of Ingolstadt*, 3

Formalism, 22, 87, 98

Frank, Rudolf, 41-42 n.33

Fuchs, Georg: *Revolution in the Theatre*, 118; *The Theatre of the Future*, 60; 123 n.2

Futurism, Russian, 22, 113 n.53

Futurism-Dynamism (French), 6 n.10

Garin, Erast, 79-80

Der Gegner, 12

Geis, Jacob, 6 n.8

Gogol, Nikolai: *The Inspector General*, 51, 69, 77, 78-83, 86, 89 n.3, 89-90 n.5, 106

Gorelik, Mordecai, 105

Griboedov, Aleksandr: *Woe to Wit*, 89

Grosz, George, 3

Guilbeaux, Henri, 3-4, 6 n.10

Hauptmann, Gerhart: *Colleague Krampton*, 51; *Schluck and Jau*, 51, 70

Holitscher, Arthur, 11-12, 38 n.9

Houghton, Norris, 62

Huppert, Hugo, 14-15

Hurwicz, Angelika, 96

Ibsen, Henrik: *An Enemy of the People*, 57; *Hedda Gabler*, 66

Ihering, Herbert, 41-42 n.33, 89

Immermann, Karl, 54-55, 73 n.24

Jessner, Leopold, 15, 54, 100, 118-19

Kamerny Theater, 14

Komissarzhevskaia, Vera, 52, 53-54, 55, 56

Komissarzhevskii, Fedor, 16

Kutscher, Artur, 7 n.10

Lacis, Anna: and children's theater, 41 n.27; on the *Inspector General* debate, 42 n.37; and *The Life of Edward II of England*, 41-42 n.33; links to German and Soviet theater, 14, 16-19, 22, 43 n.39, 49; student of Bekhterev, 40 n.22, 64; writes history of German revolutionary theater, 32

Lermontov, Mikhail: *Masquerade*, 55, 80

Ley-Piscator, Maria, 3

Das literarische Echo, 12, 38 nn.9, 11

Die literarische Welt, 12

Lukàcs, Georg, 99-100

Lunacharskaia-Rozenel', Nataliia, 47 n.76, 77

Lunacharsky, Anatoly: and Brecht, 47 n.77, 96; lectures in

Germany, 11; and Meyerhold, 45-46 n.64, 46 n.68; Soviet and German theater, 14, 30-33, 34

Maeterlinck, Maurice: *Death of Tintagiles*, 50, 70; *Pelleas and Melisande* 54; *Seven Princesses*, 71; *Sister Beatrice*, 66
Malevich, Kasimir, 56
Mann, Thomas, 93, 96
Marinetti, Filippo T., 67, 76 n.73, 103
Marlowe, Christopher: *Edward II*, 91-93, 94-95
Martinet, Marcel: *La Nuit*. See Tretiakov, Sergei: *The Earth Rampant*
Mayakovsky, Vladimir: *The Bathhouse*, 83-85; *The Bedbug*, 15, 51, 86-87; *Mystery-Bouffe*, 2-3, 51, 56
Mei Lan-fang, 22-24, 102, 112 n.51
Meyerhold, Vsevolod E.: on actors and acting, 1-2, 14, 62-67; agitprop theater, 17, 32; and V. M. Bekhterev, 40-41 n.22; biomechanics, 20, 35, 63; and Brecht, 1, 3-5, 9; *commedia dell'arte*, 12; "conscious" theater, 12, 50 60-61; Constructivism in theatre, 57; crowded setting, 80-81; Cubism in theater, 56, 57; episodic structure, 12, 55-56, 77-78, 79, 89, 113 n.58; fame in Germany, 3-4, 6 n.10, 38 n.8; use of film, 68, 77; Formalism, 111 n.29; gestic techniques, 12, 66-68, 79, 88; the grotesque, 61, 66, 78; hallmark devices, 36, 38 n.10, 52-54; Impressionist devices, 50-51; with Vera Komissarzhev-

skaia, 52-53; lighting for stage, 53, 108-9; and Lunacharsky, 30-31; and Mei Lan-fang, 23-24, 102; montage theater, 53, 61-62, 75 n.47, 77-78; at the Moscow Art Theater, 1, 50-51; use of music, 70-71 87-88; and Nemirovich-Danchenko, 1; oriental devices, 12, 65; painting for theater, 12, participatory audience, 52, 54-55, 70, 74 n.41, 83-84, 87-88, 103, 108, 119; political theater, 57-60; pre-acting, 35, 82; rational theater, 63; realism vs. stylization, 88; "rehabilitation" of, 120; "social mask" theater, 107-8; stage settings, 54-55, 72 n.7, 105-6; stage staircase, 119; stylization in theater, 51; Symbolist drama, 39 n.13, 49-56, 58, 71, 72 n.3, 93, 106; text adaptation and reinterpretation, 1, 6 n.10, 68-70, 75 n.71, 77-78, 79, 80, 85-87; tour in Germany, 3-4, 11, 13, 14, 40 n.19; and Evgenii Vakhtangov, 48 n.81; in *Das Wort*, 36. Works and productions: *Adoration of the Cross*, 53, 55; *The Bathhouse*, 83-85; *The Bedbug*, 51, 86-87; *Camille*, 51, 53, 62; *Colleague Krampton*, 51; *The Dawns*, 60, 69; *Death of Tintagiles*, 50, 70; *Don Juan*, 59; *The Earth Rampant*, 11, 53, 68, 71, 76 n.75; *Electra*, 16; *Eternal Fairy Tale*, 56; *The Fairground Booth*, 66, 103; *The Forest*, 11, 12, 53, 61-62, 65, 75 n.49, 77-78; *The Hostages of Life*, 16; *The Inspector General*, 18-19, 42 n.37, 51, 77, 78-83, 86, 89, 89 n.3, 89-90 n.5, 106; *The Life of a Man*, 53, 55; *The Love of Three Oranges* (journal), 16, 41 n.24; *The Magnanimous Cuckold*, 11, 57, 65; *Masquerade*, 55, 80; *Mid-Channel*, 16; *Mystery-Bouffe*, 51, 56-57; *Pelleas and Melisande*, 54; *The Queen of Spades*, 51; *Roar, China!*, 11, 12, 13-14; *Schluck and Jau*, 51, 70; *Sister Beatrice*, 66; *Spring's Awakening*, 53, 61; *Teacher Bubus*, 11, 31-32, 71; *Trust D. E.*, 11, 57, 68, 77, 96, 106; *The Unknown Woman*, 53, 61; *Victory of Death*, 54; *The Warrant*, 31-32; *Woe to Wit*, 23, 69, 89

Molière, Jean Baptiste: *Don Juan*, 59, 97-98

Montage, in theater, 75 n.47, 77

Moscow Art Theater, 109

Moscow Art Theater Studio, 53-54

Moscow Yiddish Theater, 107

Munich *Kammerspiele*, 17-18, 41-42 n.33, 49, 106

Neher, Caspar, 3, 93, 105, 107

Die neue Rundschau, 39 n.9

Das neue Russland, 11, 38 n.8

Okhlopkov, Nikolai, 15, 36, 39-40 n.18

Ostranenie, 44 n.46. *See also* V-Effect

Ostrovsky, Aleksandr: *The Forest*, 12, 53, 61-62, 65, 77-78, 96

Otchuzhdenie, 44 n.46. *See also* V-Effect

Paquet, Alfons: *Flags*, 68; *The Tidal Wave*, 68

Piscator, Erwin: and Brecht, 35, 43 n.44; and S. Dudow, 15;

epic theater, 48 n.86; use of film, 68; global setting, 73 n.32; hallmark devices, 68; and Soviet theater, 3, 6-7, .10, 14-15, 117; text adaptation, 69. Productions: *Flags*, 68; *Hooray, We're Alive*, 73 n.32; *Die Räuber*, 6 n.10; *The Tidal Wave*, 68

Prokofiev, Sergei: 86; *The Love of Three Oranges*, 41 n.24

Proletkult Theater, 110 n.8

Przybyszewski, Stanislaw: *Eternal Fairy Tale*, 56

Raikh, Zinaida, 33

Reich, Bernahrd, 12, 14, 17-18, 19, 36, 49, 89, 120

Rodyekno, Peter, 112 n.51

Die rote Fahne, 12

Russian and Soviet culture and art, influence in Germany, 9-13

Sapunov, Nikolai, 50

Schnitzler, Arthur: *The Cry of Life*, 66

Serban, Andrei, 122-23

Shklovsky, Viktor, 22, 44 nn.46, 47, 49

Sologub, Fedor: *Death's Victory*, 54, 119

Stanislavsky, Konstantin: article on, in *Das Wort*, 36; and *The Inspector General*, 79; Moscow Art Theater, first German tour, 12; and Symbolist theater, 50, 72 n.2; training actors, 62, 64, 100

Strindberg, August: *A Dream Play*, 113 n.58

Strittmatter, Erwin: *Katzgraben*, 108

Sudeikin, Sergei, 50

Symbolist drama, 49-53, 71, 72
    n.2, 77, 106

Tairov, Aleksandr, 3, 4, 6 n.9, 7
    n.10, 12-13, 39 n.13
Theater Union (New York), 105
Tolstoy, Alexei, 68, 73 n.32
Tomashevsky, Boris, 113 n.53
TRAM (Young Workers' Thea-
    ter), 32, 46 n.74
Tretiakov, Sergei: arrest and exe-
    cution, 33; and Brecht, 14, 43
    nn.39, 43, 44, 44 n.47, 45 n.58;
    connections to German and
    Soviet theater, 11, 14, 19-22,
    24; dialectic or "new" drama,
    27, 113 n.55; and Lukàcs, 99;
    and Mei Lan-fang, 102; and
    Meyerhold, 20, 24, 43 n.43,
    103. Works: Den Shi-hua, 23;
    The Earth Rampant, (from mar-
    cel Martinet, La Nuit), 11, 53,
    68, 71, 76 n.75; Field Marshals,
    26, 27-29, 45 n.58; I Want a

Baby, 26-27, 43 n.43, 45 nn.58,
    60, 72 nn.7, 13, 82-88; Roar,
    China! 11, 13-14, 23, 39 n.16,
    89

Vakhtangov, Evgenii, 35, 36, 39
    n.13, 48 n.1
Vakhtangov Theater, 12, 14
Varlamov, Konstantin, 59, 60
V-Effect (Verfremdung), 21-22, 35,
    44 nn.46, 49, 102-3, 112 n.51
Verhaeren, Emile: The Dawns, 53,
    60, 69

Wedekind, Frank: Spring's Awak-
    ening, 53, 61
Weigel, Helene, 75 n.54, 100, 112
    n.39
Weill, Kurt, 31, 32
Die Weltbühne, 13
Das Wort, 36-37, 46-47 n.76, 99

Zuckmayer, Carl, 10

About the Author

KATHERINE BLISS EATON is Associate Professor of English at Tarrant County Junior College in Fort Worth. Her articles have been published in both European and American journals.